Judy Moody

Career Decisions in Computer Technology Fields

Judy Moody

Career Decisions in Computer Technology Fields

Influences, Barriers, and Gender Issues

VDM Verlag Dr. Müller

Imprint

Bibliographic information by the German National Library: The German National Library lists this publication at the German National Bibliography; detailed bibliographic information is available on the Internet at http://dnb.d-nb.de.

Cover image: www.purestockx.com

Publisher:
VDM Verlag Dr. Müller Aktiengesellschaft & Co. KG , Dudweiler Landstr. 125 a,
66123 Saarbrücken, Germany,
Phone +49 681 9100-698, Fax +49 681 9100-988,
Email: info@vdm-verlag.de

Zugl.: Stillwater, Oklahoma State University, Diss., 2006

Produced in USA and UK by:
Lightning Source Inc., La Vergne, Tennessee, USA
Lightning Source UK Ltd., Milton Keynes, UK
BookSurge LLC, 5341 Dorchester Road, Suite 16, North Charleston, SC 29418, USA

ISBN: 978-3-639-01892-9

TABLE OF CONTENTS

LIST OF TABLES

LIST OF FIGURES

CHAPTER I

INTRODUCTION

Introduction: From Researcher's Perspective

"What do you want to be when you grow up?" is a question that is asked of children throughout their childhood. Some adults hear that question all their lives, because they have a difficult time deciding on a career and continually change professions throughout their careers.

Most adults work the majority of their lives, so their career choices are important and many times affect their life styles. The type of work a person chooses will provide rewards and present limitations to the quality of life, such as housing, clothing, vehicles, vacations, and hobbies. Career choices affect salaries, co-workers, and job satisfaction that sometimes affect happiness.

Career decisions are affected by a number of things. One factor is timing. A person's year of birth determines job availability. Jobs such as blacksmithing are limited today, and computer jobs were not available until the twentieth century because there were no computers. Moreover, the location of birth affects job selections. A child is less likely to become a ski jumper if born in Oklahoma than if born in Switzerland. Furthermore, who the parents are also has an effect on the child's career opportunities. Children from privileged backgrounds have an opportunity to experience rich educational and personal occurrences that children from less privileged homes might not experience.

Additionally, parents that are actors, doctors, lawyers, and other professions provide an example and sometimes encourage their children to follow in parental footsteps, thus influencing career decisions. Finally, teachers, ministers, and other adults with whom children spend time, provide an example for children, give exposure to a variety of careers, and have an influence on career decisions. Friends also have an impact on people of all ages, but certainly at a young age. Friends encourage friends to join the military, select certain post-secondary schools, not attend school, or other post high school life decisions.

Physical attributes, intelligence level, race, and gender are all precipitators of career and educational choices. Additionally, job characteristics such as salary, working conditions, co-workers, and location affect career decisions. Combined with a multitude of other dynamics, the afore-mentioned factors are influences and, in some cases, barriers to occupational choices.

Career choices affect a person's life in so many ways. Those decisions should be considered a major step in life. The researcher was recruited in high school to pursue a computer technology career. Although personal computer experience has enhanced job opportunities and continues to be an important asset in the workplace, the researcher wonders how outside influences altered her own career path. A personal belief in the importance of career choices and personal experience with the influences and barriers that can impact choice of career in computing, particularly for women, provided strong impetus for this study.

Background and Theoretical Framework

This study was framed and supported by several historical perspectives and theoretical components.

Historical Perspective on Career Preparation

Philosophies about work and preparing for work have changed over time, but beliefs from ancient Greece and Rome have influenced prejudices about work and education that have survived over the centuries. As civilizations formed, workers became skilled in an area and mentored students to take their place in the tribe as a medicine doctor or hunter. As communities grew, new professions emerged. Most people learned a trade or profession by working with their parents or a mentor, thus limiting opportunities for some. During that time, only the wealthy or privileged people attended formal school, and the majority of individuals were uneducated until recent times. In numerous countries, thousands of people are still uneducated because of access restrictions (Gray & Herr, 1998).

Historically some tension has existed regarding the role and focus of education for workforce preparation. "The advocates of liberal education have stressed the training of minds over the demands of preparing people for jobs and careers" (Elias & Merriam, 1998, p. 18). However, the "role of workforce education related to providing career opportunity for individuals, is to provide programs of study designed to prepare individuals to 'enter' the labor market" (Gray & Herr, 1998, pp. 30-31).

Gender has played a part in labor division throughout human history. "Beliefs about differences between the sexes, many of them taken as axiomatic, play an important role in the organization of social life" (Reskin & Hartman, 1986, p. 38). The major

3

concentration of a dominant sex in different jobs has been labeled sex segregation in the

labor market, and surprisingly the overall degree of sex segregation has been stable since

1900 (Reskin & Hartman, 1986). The following summarizes the gender dilemma in

occupational markets:

> In the past women have not had equal opportunity in the labor market, and
> they have faced discrimination in hiring, pay, and advancement. To some
> extent the differences in women's and men's earnings and in the
> occupations they hold reflect that past discrimination; to some extent they
> reflect current discrimination, and to some extent they reflect a host of
> other factors, such as differences between women and men in their
> preferences, attitudes, values, experience, education, training, and so on.
> And it is highly likely that all these factors are interrelated (Reskin &
> Hartman, 1986, p. 2).

The historical differences in opportunities for men and women suggested to the

researcher that the genders might report different barriers and influences in choosing

careers in the computer field. Philosophically, occupational education is grounded in

equity of gender access across career fields. "Some of the basic principles in adult

education originated in progressive thought" (Elias & Merriam, 1998, p. 45) and include

equal educational opportunity. Progressive philosophies supported social change and

encouraged females to become active in politics to help promote social change.

Progressive thinkers believed everyone had unlimited potential that could be developed

through education. Democracy meant that it was society's responsibility to provide an

education for everyone, including females (Gray & Herr, 1998). However, the reality has

been somewhat different, and "thirty years after enactment of Title IX, the patterns of

enrollment in vocational and technical programs look shockingly similar to the patterns

that existed prior to passage of the law" (National Women's Law Center, 2002, p. 4). The

Center's investigations also discovered that females who enroll in a traditional female

4

program "have fewer opportunities to take advanced level classes" (p. 5) or enroll in computer technology programs. This reality supports the researcher's substantive hypothesis that influences and barriers to careers in computing may be different for males and females.

Also historically related to career choices are career guidance models. "Contemporary forms of career guidance in the United States originated in the models of vocational guidance that arose in the late nineteenth and early twentieth centuries as a partner to vocational education" (Gray & Herr, 1998, p. 215). As the nature of vocational education changed, career guidance gained a relationship to gender. When vocational training became part of the liberal arts schools, there was concern about education for females, because it highlighted limited choices to enroll in vocational programs (Elias & Merriam, 1998).

Career choices and educational development have historically concentrated on problems that people experience as they choose, train, enter, and adapt to work (Gray & Herr, 1998). Those problems include gender equity and the variance of male/female needs, interests, and experiences and were key elements in career decisions. Technology changed the world and become an influence to career choices, which focused on altering relationships between the genders and between gender and technology (isi.salford.ac.uk, 2006).

Career models profile a description of the area of responsibility, the know-how, experiences, and skills required for positions to provide prospects of employment. When using a career model, it does not matter whether students are at the start of their career or seeking orientation for new development targets (Read, 2002). The traditional career

5

models have used developmental stages, academic learning, employable skills, and lifelong learning as deciders (Brown, 2003; Wickwire, 2001). Those career models suggested that employees would train and remain in a selected career field. By contrast, more current career models have stressed income, status, power, and security (Brown, 2003). Successful employees are characterized as mobile, flexible, team players, and technological (Read, 2002).

Importance of Computer Careers in Today's Workforce

"As the world of work has evolved, so has the way individuals are functioning in the workplace, requiring new forms of workforce preparation" (Brown, 2003, p. 1). Since the beginning of civilization when man began making tools, humans have invented and used tools to assist in the performance of tasks. Those inventions were sometimes referred to as technical innovations. Technical jobs increased during the American industrial revolution between 1870 and 1906 (Gray & Herr, 1998) and continue to increase today. Since technology, especially in the form of computers, has become such a large component of everyday life, everyone benefits by obtaining experience with and knowledge of computers. Computer jobs vary in salary depending on the position, and the job rankings list many computer professionals in the top 50 paying occupations. "In addition to the high earning potential, a technology career can be both personally and professionally rewarding in that it is mentally stimulating and offers numerous opportunities for advancement" (Verbick, 2002, p. 248).

Computer science degrees and computer jobs were limited or non-existent until the eighties and nineties. Today technology has expanded into almost every profession, and universities now offer technology degrees in several forms. In fact, technology

6

classes are mandated as a part of many other degrees. The importance of computing careers and computing skills in today's workforce led this researcher to believe that a study of influences and barriers in selecting these careers was important in understanding current career climates.

Gender Inequity in Computer Careers

Typically, females have been under represented in this important career field. Wakefield (2003) wrote that despite government and industry efforts to alleviate the problem of recruiting and retaining females in technology jobs, the numbers remain low and in some cases are decreasing. Gurian and Stevens (2004) claimed that inovated education efforts would be needed to encourage females to major in technology fields, stating that, "Educators will need to provide girls with extra encouragement and gender-specific strategies to successfully engage them in spatial abstracts, including computer design" (p. 7). Henderson and Robertson (1999) alleged that most of the current career choice theories used in career education had not been developed to target career choice processes for females and minorities. This situation suggested to the researcher that a study of factors influencing female choices of careers in computing would make an important contribution to current career selection theory and practice.

Despite targeted recruitment of females, female participation has remained low in comparison to male participation in computing careers since their inception. Since the early seventies, females have been recruited by universities and companies to train in technology fields. However, few females chose careers involving computers (Verbick, 2002). Much is being done to recruit females into the technology fields. Massachusetts Institute of Technology, Harvard, and other universities offer scholarships and special classes for females majoring in math, science, and technology. However, despite this targeted recruitment, the number of females is still considerably less than males in these major areas. Several important factors may be contributing to this situation.

"From infancy through early childhood, girls receive messages that mathematics, science and technology are male domains" (p. 2), and "there is a direct correlation between a child's early learning experiences and later achievement in mathematics, science and technology" (Strauss, Shaffer, Kaser & Shaw, 1991, p. 2). Vygotsky's (1986) social development theories provided a critical frame of reference for career and technical education for understanding the perceptions of females about computer technology careers. According to Vygotsky, social interaction plays a huge role in the development of cognition through reciprocal interaction between cognitive, behavioral, an environmental influences (Riddle, 1999). When social experiences and messages are negative, this can have a strong impact on career decisions.

Studies have indicated that in school and the workplace, gender bias has inhibited females from reaching their full potential in math, science and technology (Strauss, Shaffer, Kaser & Shaw, 1991). Harassment in non-traditional classes, incomplete information, poor counseling, and the lack of role models have also driven women toward traditional female programs (National Women's Law Center, 2002). By the time females attend college, they have experienced less computing opportunities than males.

Females were often hindered by computer-science curricula, which assumed students had some knowledge of the field and focused on the computer as a tool to solve all problems. While schools offer more courses in technology, few females have elected to enroll in the classes (National Women's Law Center, 2002). According to the

8

Association of University Women (AAUW) (2000), women receive less that 28% of the computer science bachelor degrees. This under representation of women in computing fields will have a negative impact on the economy around the world (U.S. Department of Labor, 2000). In addition, "75% of new jobs will require use of computers, but only 33% of females enroll in computer related courses" (National Women's Law Center, 2002, p. 6).

Taken collectively, the research evidence suggests that gender inequity is still present in computing careers and that this situation may negatively impact the American workforce. This led this researcher to conclude that different influences and barriers may be operating between the genders in making a decision to undertake a career in a computing field, and that an analysis of these gender choice dynamics could be useful in targeting future career choice counseling and recruitment.

Career Selection Models

Career development is more than finding and training for a job. There is a distinction between occupation and career. What job is performed is the occupation and the career is the course followed throughout a lifetime (Gray & Herr, 1998). Career selection theories are grounded in human development theories. Psychologists have agreed that choosing a career is a developmental process, but psychologists have posited varying theories that are classified as structural, developmental, and social learning perspectives on career selection (Jespen, 1984).

Career theories from the *structural perspective* described personality traits in individuals and match the traits to the job. Personality differences such as interests and abilities developed from early childhood and grown throughout life help structure personality characteristics (Jespen, 1984). In structural career choice models, factors such as personal values and personality characteristics must be considered in order to fit occupations to individuals (Gray & Herr, 1998).

Developmental career theory focused on the differences in the person as he/she matures. Time changes the person, and developmental career theory deals with personal change when choosing, entering, and progressing in work roles. The developmental perspective includes distinguishable views about behavioral change over time (Jespen, 1984). It includes "readiness to cope with the developmental tasks of one's life stage, to make socially required career decisions, and to cope appropriately with the tasks society confronts the developing youth and adults" (Super & Jordaan, 1973, p. 4). In developmental models, various developmental tasks should be explored at different chronological ages to develop effective career decision making skills (Gray & Herr, 1998).

Another theory of career development is the *social learning theory* of career decision making, which is the interaction between the individual and the environment. This theory indicated that career behavior changes the interaction of the individuals and the environment over time. Life itself is a series of changing environments and roles that change as a result of finding new things about ourselves as time goes on (Tiedeman, 1999). In the social learning model, career counseling has both internal elements such as individual ability and individual needs as well as external elements such as societal forces (Campbell, Walz, Miller, & Kriger, 1973).

However, these traditional models may be somewhat outdated and may not be relevant to trends in computing career selection. Woodard (2005) found that baby boomers did not follow standard career choice models. This led this researcher to wonder if traditional career selection models may also be inadequate to explain influences and barriers that impact decisions to enter a career in technology fields, and particularly potential gender differences in these influences and barriers.

Unique, gender – specific influences and barriers may be driving a career selection model that contributes to the problem of the lack of females in computer technology fields. Those influences and barriers may sway some females negatively, thus limiting the technological job pool. Without clear identification of these negative influences, it is not possible to develop sound strategies to address them and increase female participation in the technology workforce.

Statement of the Problem

According to the Bureau of Labor Statistics, in 2001 women represented over forty-six (46) percent of the total workforce, but less than twenty-five (25) percent of the professional technology workforce (Verbick, 2002). Although America promotes democratic equality in workforce education (Gray & Herr, 1998), there are fewer females than males majoring in technology occupations, thus creating an inconsistency of theory and practice. The contradictions between those beliefs and actuality are a problem that America and other countries recognize and are taking action to facilitate social change to balance gender issues in technology. Traditional career selection models may be inadequate to explain the influences and barriers that affect decisions to enter a career in computing, and particularly gender – based differences in these factors. There currently exists no clear data on these career decision dynamics, and without such data, sound career guidance procedures to address the computer technology fields cannot be developed.

Purpose of the Study

The purpose of this study was to analyze career decisions in technology and related gender differentiation. Specifically, the study met four purposes: (1) describe and compare profiles of students majoring in computer technology programs to non-technology students and compare female to male students, (2) describe influences and barriers on career decisions for computer technology students and compare to non-technology students, (3) compare gender influences/barriers patterns for computer technology students and compare to non-technology students, and (4) compare the career choice model generated by this study to traditional models. The general goal of this study was to gain more understanding of the decision making process of selecting a major in a technology field and create a building block for more research and understanding of female recruitment in technology fields.

Research Questions

This study was guided by five research questions:

1. What is the demographic profile of students who pursue careers in computer technology and how does it compare with non-technology career clusters?

2. Are those demographic profiles the same for males and females?

3. What is the profile of influences and barriers for students who pursue careers in computer technology and how does it compare with non-technology career clusters?

4. Are those influences the same for male and female students?

5. How does the model identified in this study for choosing a computer technology career compare to existing career choice models?

The five research questions for this study were addressed with descriptive statistics. As shown in Table 1, the first question was addressed with a profile construction based on obtained frequencies, percentages, and cross-tabulation obtained from a questionnaire developed for this study. The third question dealt with influences and barriers to computing career choices, based on questionnaire items and descriptive statistics. The second and fourth questions compare the responses of females and males, using descriptive statistics for group comparison. The fifth question compared a career selection model generated by the study's findings to existing career choice models.

Table 1

Research Questions, Data Source, and Data Analysis

Research Question	Data Source	Data Analysis
1. What is the demographic profile of students who pursue careers in computer technology and how does it compare with non-technology career clusters?	Questionnaire responses to questions 1-16.	Descriptive Statistics and cross-tabulation.
2. Are those demographic profiles the same for male and female students?	Questionnaire responses to questions 1-16.	Descriptive Statistics and cross-tabulation.
3. What is the profile of influences and barriers for students who pursue careers in computer technology and how does it compare with non-technology career clusters?	Questionnaire responses to questions 17- 60.	Descriptive Statistics and cross-tabulation.

4. Are those influences the same for male and female students?	Questionnaire responses to questions 17- 60.	Descriptive Statistics and cross-tabulation.
5. How does the model identified in this study for choosing a computer technology career compare to existing career choice models?	All questionnaire responses.	Logic analysis of question responses.

Definitions of Key Terms

The following definitions were used in this study and were obtained from the

American Heritage® Dictionary of the English Language, fourth edition (2005).

Conceptual Definitions

Career: The general course or progression of one's working life or one's

professional achievements.

Discrimination: Treatment or consideration based on class or category rather

than individual merit; partiality or prejudice.

Emancipation: To free from bondage, oppression, or restraint; liberate.

"Geek" Image: A person who is single-minded or accomplished in scientific or

technical pursuits but is felt to be socially inept.

Gender: A grammatical category used in the classification of nouns, pronouns,

adjectives, and, in some languages, verbs that may be arbitrary or based on

characteristics such as sex and that determines agreement with or selection of

modifiers, referents, or grammatical forms.

Oppressed: Kept down by severe and unjust use of force or authority.

Technology: The application of science, especially to industrial or commercial objectives.

Career-decision efficacy: Power or capacity to make decisions about a career.

Operational Definitions

Career clusters: Occupational groupings of specific industry based jobs for student selection at the Oklahoma Career and Technology Centers. These 16 clusters represent all career possibilities and are listed as: Agriculture, Food, & Natural Resources; Architecture & Construction; Arts, A/V Technology & Communications; Business, Management & Administration; Education & Training; Finance; Government & Public Administration; Health Science; Hospitality & Tourism; Human Services; Information Technology; Law, Public Safety & Security; Manufacturing; Marketing, Sales & Service; Science, Technology, Engineering & Mathematics; and Transportation, Distribution & Logistics (CareerTech, 2004).

CareerTech: Oklahoma's Department of Career and Technology Education that offers comprehensive statewide programs for career and technology education, governed by the State Board of Career and Technology Education.

Computer technology career: Enrollment in an Oklahoma Technology Center in a program in one of the following Career Clusters: Arts, A/V Technology and Communications; Information Technology; and Science, Technology, Engineering, and Mathematics.

Oklahoma technology center: An educational facility that provides workforce training in 29 technology center districts operating on 55 campuses, 398 comprehensive school districts, 25 skill centers and three juvenile facilities.

Standard career models: Career models based on developmental stages, interest, and aptitude.

Influences and barriers: Responses on a questionnaire requiring forced demographic choices response and selections of a 5-point Likert scale.

Methodology

General Approach

This study was descriptive in approach. Descriptive research describes existing conditions and enables the researcher to meaningfully describe data with numerical indices or graphic form (Fraenkel & Wallen, 2003), which was the goal of this study. The five research questions guiding this study gathered information from student responses to a structured-response questionnaire. The online questionnaire was used to collect demographic data and information about influences and barriers when making decisions about selecting a career. The information was then used to determine if the selection process varied for males and females. The study was used to gain more understanding of the decision making process of selecting a major in a computer technology field.

Population and Sample

Researchers prefer to study the entire population of interest (Fraenkel & Wallen, 2003), but it is not feasible to survey everyone that has ever made a career decision or even everyone in Oklahoma who has made such a decision. The population of interest for this study was current students that are 18 years of age or older attending one of the 29 Technology Centers in the Oklahoma CareerTech system at 55 campus locations throughout the state. It was impossible to survey even this delimited population, thus necessitating use of a sample.

16

"Samples should be as large as a researcher can obtain with a reasonable expenditure of time and energy. A recommended minimum number of subjects is one hundred (100) for a descriptive study, fifty (50) for a correlational study, and thirty (30) in each group for experimental and causal-comparative studies" (Fraenkel & Wallen, 2003, p. 113). Traveling to numerous locations to collect data by personal interviews or written questionnaires would be time consuming and expensive. The telephone, mail, and Internet have been used in many studies to help alleviate those restraints. However, contacting participants by phone, through the mail, and on the Internet sometimes limits sample participation because of lack of personal contact (Evensen, 2005), which can bias a self-selected sample such as the one in this study. This introduced a limitation of the study, but certainly did not prevent its conduct.

The obtained sample for this study was a self-selected convenience sample, defined as all members of the target population who completed and submitted the online questionnaire (N=424). The sampling was also purposive based on the fact that all students at the Technology Centers have made decisions about the pursuit of a career in a career cluster and had exposure to computers at the Technology Centers.

Instrumentation

A questionnaire was selected as the preferred type of data collection for this study because of reaching the maximum number of students in a timely manner and at a minimum expense for the amount of information gathered. Presenting the questionnaire online provided access to a larger sample and guaranteed anonymity for the subjects. The proper steps and references were made to insure reliability and validity of the questionnaire instrument, as discussed in Chapter III. The questionnaire was divided into three sections. The responses to the questionnaire yielded individual scores that were used for descriptive data analysis, including measures of central tendency, measures of dispersion, and cross-tabulation.

Procedures

Information was sent to the student services coordinators/program directors at 55 Oklahoma Technology Center campuses recruiting their assistance in informing and encouraging eligible CareerTech students to participate. The questionnaire web site was made available to campus coordinators and CareerTech teachers for preview prior to student availability. There was no direct interaction by the researcher with participants or teachers. The data were submitted online, compiled in a data file, and then exported to the Statistical Package for the Social Sciences (SPSS).

Data Analysis

The responses to the sixty survey questions yielded a frequency number and a percentage for career influences and barriers and categorical variables of gender and technology or non-technology careers. These data were used for descriptive, comparative analyses.

Assumptions of the Study

The following assumptions were made regarding the participants of the study:

1) Students have made some decisions about their career choices.

2) Students have been influenced and are aware of those factors that have influenced their career decisions.

3) Students were honest in their responses.

4) Students living with parents provided accurate income information.

18

Limitations of the Study

The following limitations due to certain drawbacks to questionnaire research were inherent in this study:

1. Response by participants was voluntary, which could have limited both size and representativeness of the obtained sample.

2. Another possible limitation was that respondents may not have fully understand a question and needed clarification which was unavailable to them.

3. Self reporting was also a limitation because there may have been misunderstandings of questions or deliberately falsified information provided.

4. Participants' preconceived notions about computers may also have skewed the responses.

5. Another limitation was in using a Likert scaled questionnaire that could allow participants to report more neutral responses by straddling the fence (Brown, 2003). However, the Likert scale did allow participants to report indecision or a weak stance as opposed to a yes or no response, thus lessening the impacts of this limitation.

Delimitations of the Study

Delimitations of the study were that it included only students over the age of 18 in the state of Oklahoma, and only students at the CareerTech Technology Centers. Students in high schools, universities, and people not currently attending school were not included. This placed limits on the generalizability of the findings beyond the Career Tech sector or beyond the state of Oklahoma.

Significance of the Study

Decisions are influenced by internal and external factors. Influences and barriers on career decisions begin at a very early age with and without conscious effort or recognition by the individual or by the influencer. Awareness and understanding of those influences and barriers may help people make more appropriate career choices.

There is a lack of gender equality in many professions. Equal opportunity supporters have encouraged men and women to enter fields in which they have previously faced discrimination. Over the past few years more males have become elementary school teachers, nurses, and manicurists, while more females have become doctors, lawyers, and corporate managers than in the past. However, technology is a profession that remains dominated by males (Cavanagh, 2002). Gregory Andrews (2004), National Science Foundation (NSF) division director, said in a news brief that, "The lack of women in information technology (IT) reduces the nation's technological workforce, hinders women's economic advancement, and undermines the creativity and success of the IT industry" (¶ 4). Thus, it can be argued that male domination negatively influences female participation in education for technology careers and consequently reduces female participation in the available technology career labor pool. This study profiled students who are entering computer technology careers, described influences and barriers to selecting or rejecting a computer technology career, and compared those factors for males and females. This information may provide guidance to better understand the dynamics of career decisions in an economically important career field, help eliminate participation barriers, enlighten influencers to increase the opportunities for females to pursue computer technology careers, increase their economic potential, and broaden the

available labor pool in this critical occupational field for the Information Age.

CHAPTER II

REVIEW OF LITERATURE

Careers

Definition of Careers

The general succession of the work history or professional accomplishments of an individual is one's career (Katz, 1992). Usually a career is thought of as a permanent occupation or lifework such as an officer with a distinguished career or a teacher at the end of a long career. Other career definition examples are career diplomats and career criminals, implying that the career spanned over a long period of time (American Heritage, n.d.). Gray & Herr (1998) stated that, "Careers are longitudinal, they occur across the life span, and they include the various jobs, occupations, educational, prevocational and postvocational roles in which the individual engages" (pp. 114-115).

A chosen profession defines our status in life in many ways financially, personally, socially, and academically (Katz, 1992). Some professions can be financially rewarding but not socially acceptable, such as illegal professions. Others could be legal and financially rewarding but not socially perceived as prestigious jobs, such as plumbers, and maintenance workers. Some professions are socially acceptable such as teachers, nurses, and secretaries, but are not as financially rewarding. Other professions are academically challenging but not personally rewarding. "The connections between career, motivation, and self-worth are assumed to be reciprocal and interactive" (Gray &

22

Herr, 1998, p. 115). Whatever career one chooses can define their life (Taylor, 1948).

Career and Education

Early philosophies of education assumed there was a division between education and work; however, a continuous lifetime career is now a thing of the past and learning can no longer be divided into school and the workplace (Fischer, 1996). The National Women's Law Center (2000) supported a unified approach to career development, claiming that, "Career education programs, such as vocational training programs, internships, and on-the-job training, are an important way for you to gain the skills you need in order to get a good job with good pay" (p. 3). Elias & Merriam (1998) suggested that adult education principles could also contribute to lifetime learning, and that "Adult education has advanced to the point where a more systematic investigation of philosophies of adult education is both possible and necessary" (pp. 11-12).

The separation of education and work is no longer possible for several reasons. First, the "intent of such programs is to provide enrollees with specific occupational skills that will give them an advantage to compete for employment" (Gray & Herr, 1998, p. 31). Second, professional activity has become so knowledge-intensive that learning has become an important part of adult work activities. "Blue-collar workers are being replaced by information specialists called knowledge workers or 'gold-collar' workers" (Brown, 1999, p. 1). Knowledge workers are recognized by employers as having a competitive edge (Overtoom, 2000), and former U.S. Secretary of Labor Reich reported that "the responsibility for preparing students and unskilled workers with the technical and cognitive skills required for 'knowledge' work" (Brown, 1999, p. 3) is in the hands of education.

Another link between education and work is that the workplace of the present and future demands a new kind of worker. Basic reading and arithmetic abilities are not enough (Hancock, 2004). As early as 1909, U. S. education and labor leaders were looking for ways to connect schools and the workplace (Hoye & Drier, 1999). For the individual worker, the workplace has become a place of cataclysmic change and untold opportunity. In the global marketplace, data is presented in picoseconds and gigabits. Adapting to a rapidly changing work environment will mean multiple career and job changes and continual learning (Peck, 1996).

One important educational need in modern work places is computer skills. Workers now need a firm foundation in computing skills as well as expertise in technical skills. In a survey about computer needs by Quinley and Hickman (2002), computer-related training was the number one training listed as needed, with eighty percent of employers reported that training was "needed" or "much needed." Computer skills and using those skills to process data in the information age were frequently noted in written comments. Fischer (1996) discussed the dichotomies in workplaces and society, stating that "Many different technical cultures exist today: novices versus skilled workers; software developers versus software users; industry people versus academics; and committed technophiles versus determined technophobes" (p. 12).

Computer Technology Careers and Computing Skills in the Workplace

Computer Technology Careers

In the past, many curriculum discussions and employment reports attempted to merge such disciplines as computer science, computer engineering, and software engineering into a single statement about computing education. While such an approach

24

may have seemed reasonable in the past, it is now clear that computing in the 21st century encompasses many different disciplines with their own identity and pedagogical traditions (Fischer, 1996). Thus, "computer technology careers" now appear to be multi-faceted rather than monolithic. Professional careers in the various fields that now make up "computer technology" offer both social approval and economic rewards. They can appeal to and be worthwhile for both old and young workers, and to both males and females. Verbick (2002) stated that "technology jobs lead to educational and economic opportunities and should not be limited to or focused toward a very select few of mostly males. Brock (2002) concurred, claiming that in addition to high earning potential, technology careers can be both personally and professionally rewarding in that they are both mentally stimulating and offer many opportunities for advancement.

Computing Skills as a Career Necessity

The rise of the Internet and its related technologies changed business and society dramatically. The resulting impact on skills required for a successful workforce was also dramatic.

The modern workplace, characterized by new technologies, equipment, communication, and management processes, requires workers to have advanced levels of job skills, including skills using information technology. Workplace education that prepares individuals with the information technology skills required for jobs in the knowledge sector has become a national priority. Brown (1999) claimed that the curricula of the schools have been altered due to the technology needs of modern workplaces and a technological society. To respond effectively to an ever-changing work and social environment, people need more than just a knowledge base. They need skills to explore,

25

make connections, and make practical use of information (Fischer, 1996). The best uses of new technologies often entail a thoughtful blending of those tools with more classical tools. Overtoom (2000) mentioned the importance of continuously honing skills past those necessary for a current job "as the key to job survival" (¶ 3).

To meet the needs of the modern workplace and its workforce, schools have been urged for more than a decade by a procession of visionaries to equip all classrooms and all students with high powered, globally connected digital tools. The demands to change our educational institutions to meet career and social needs continue to be pressing. Almost every institution is struggling with the challenges and opportunities caused by the Internet and globalization (Canton, 1999). New best practices, futurist models, visionary ideas, and educational strategies are emerging, including new ways to acquire, assimilate and share knowledge. While this is challenging, Allum (2002) claimed that institutions of learning are in a unique position to benefit from an added opportunity to provide leadership in e-knowledge.

The world as a whole took to the informational superhighway at racecar speed. The need for training a workforce to compete became apparent. Oklahoma's CareerTech System accepted this challenge and began offering training programs specifically customized to fit the unique needs of any business or industry. Recent research had indicated a major switch to business and information technology services from clerical and secretarial skills. Technology is now everywhere. It is not just in the offices and manufacturing plants, but also in beauty salons, with timing and testing chemical change in the hair; in automobiles, with digital navigation; in grocery stores, with scanning UPC; and in banks, with automated money counters (Oklahoma Department of Career and

Technology Education, n.d.). Overtoom (2002) recognized this reality in his statement that "The dual challenges of competing in a world market and rapid technological advancements have necessitated a redesign of the workplace into an innovative work environment known as the high-performance workplace" (¶ 2).

The nature of today's workplace is different from that of the past. It is characterized by global competition, cultural diversity, new technologies, and new management processes that require workers to have critical thinking, problem-solving, communication skills, advanced levels of job skills, as well as technical skills (Mehlman, 2002). David J. Pucel (1999) listed cognitive and affective skills as necessary to meet national skills standards determined by the National Skill Standards Board. The National Skill Standards Act of 1994 created the Board in a bipartisan effort in response to requests by business leaders to close the skills gap in the workplace (Allum, 2000). Within the new competitive nature of labor markets that require advanced technical and computing skills, career systems attempt to guide students to an appropriate workplace choice with an appropriate career model (Baruch, 2004). These career models have a lengthy history that extends back for over 100 years.

Career Models

Career models in use today are not new. According to Gray and Herr (1998), "Theory development and changing definitions of vocational guidance had set the stage for a transition in the terminology of the field from vocational guidance to career guidance" (p. 219). Frank Parsons, the "father of vocational guidance," developed a three-step process for vocational guidance that included opportunity and prospects in different lines of work (Gray & Herr, 1998).

When vocational education became part of liberal arts education, the education of women and their career choices became a concern because attention was called to their limited opportunities in vocational programs (Elias & Merriam, 1998). The traditional model of career education stressed a series of developmental stages, basic and academic learning, employability skill development, school and workplace linkages, as well as the need for lifelong learning and continuous skill development (Wickwire, 2001). The newer models of career education included the "new careering" which advocated a theory of life as career and focused on logical, emotional, and spiritual aspects of living (Miller-Tiedeman, 1999).

There are many types of career models ranging from linear career systems to multidirectional career systems. The Holland Hexagon Model or Holland Codes is the basis for most of the career inventories used today (Holland, 1985), and assessments using Holland Personality Styles link vocational interests to job families or career clusters. However, Kerka (1992) pointed out that "women's lives are often less linear" (¶ 4) than these theories describe, interrupted by marriage and childrearing. Kerka (1991) also asserted that non-linear models do not "follow the traditional patterns of education-work-retirement" (¶ 7) and that career changes became more socially acceptable after personal fulfillment became more valued.

Traditionalists following traditional career models take a job and remain in that position throughout their career. By contrast, non-traditional models view careers as a means of growth and workers using this model are ready for change when the job is no longer intrinsic rewarding (Kerka, 1991). The alternative models interweave the individual, family, and work so that people become empowered to construct their own

28

career destinies (Brown, 2000). "A major criticism of prevailing theories is that they are based on male experiences" (Kerka, 1992, ¶ 4).

Other models based on male experiences are person-centered, competency based, instructional, and developmental models (Bhaerman, 1988), which use individualized career plans. Those models use values, interests, personality, and skills to analyze possible careers.

Free form careers include consulting, temporary jobs, part-time jobs, or entrepreneurial activities. Mixed form models are a transition between linear and free-form patterns (Kerka, 1991).

Paulsen and Betz (2004) summarized the results of a study of over 600 students surveyed regarding predictors in making career decisions. Their study defined self-efficacy in career decision making as believing that someone was capable of making a confident, realistic decision for themselves. Career decision-making self-efficacy had received considerable attention from researchers, because of the importance of choosing a career. It had the potential for determining a person's future. Paulsen and Betz (2004) measured career efficacy "using five task domains: accurate self appraisal; occupational information; goal selection; planning; and problem solving" (p. 355). After establishing a career decision-making self-efficacy scale using those five task domains, they compared it to the confidence level in six areas of basic competencies of a liberal arts education. The "six basic confidence dimensions were Mathematics, Science, Using Technology, Writing, Leadership, and Cultural Sensitivity" (p. 356). These researchers felt that awareness of predictors of career decisions could assist college advisors in student career advisement and career intervention.

Colorado College (2006) outlined a 7-step decision-making model to choosing a course of action. Their literature states that "The effectiveness of your career decision-making relies heavily on the information available to you at the decision-making point" (¶ 1). The Colorado College career model assumes that information is powerful and that limited information often effects career making decisions and thus affects the outcome. "The trick is to figure out what information you are lacking and then gather and analyze that information" (¶ 1).

Career choices are at base an aspect of human behavior and thus have a relationship to behavioral psychology. Watson's work on human behavior was based on the experiments of Ivan Pavlov. Pavlov studied animal responses to conditioning (DeMar, 1997). Well-known behaviorist psychologist, Skinner expanded upon the work of Watson and Pavlov with his theory of Operant Conditioning and attempted to explain, control, and predict more complex human behaviors. Skinner believed that humans are controlled by their environment, the conditions of which can be studied, specified, and manipulated (Elias & Merriam, 1998). Those principles have implication for how environmental influences effect career decisions.

Career Decisions

Tomorrow's leaders, today's students learn in a fast-paced environment where they will fashion and shape those changes for the future (Brown, 1999). Some futurists have claimed that students of the future will design individualized learning programs that will increase their skills, creativity, understanding, and career choices (Canton, 1999). Choosing a career can be the most important decision in predicting an individual's future, and career changes often occur because of economic climate, technological advances, and

30

changing attitudes toward work. Finding one's own definitions or models of success in the workplace is vitally important to a successful life (Kerka, 1991).

Philosophies about work and preparing for work have changed, but Gray and Herr (1998) have pointed out several ideas from history that have influenced injustice about work and education that have survived over time. For example, in medieval times, skilled craftsmen secured their jobs by limiting the supply of trained craftsmen. Most people learned a trade by working with their parents or a mentor, thus limiting opportunity for some. Until relatively recently, only the wealthy attended formal school and the majority of people remained uneducated.

The School-to-Work Opportunities Act combines school and learning a trade in a modern age. The act prepares students for their first job by integrating academic and occupational learning by establishing a link from secondary schools to post-secondary schools. "The act also defines 'career guidance and counseling' to mean" (Gray & Herr, 1998, p. 225) techniques used to develop "career awareness, career planning, career decision making, placement skills, and knowledge and understanding of local, state and national occupation, education, and labor market needs, trends, and opportunities" (p. 226). It also assists students in making informed occupational choices and aids students in developing career options "surrounding gender, race, ethnic, disability, language, or socioeconomic impediments to career options and encouraging careers in nontraditional employment" (p. 226).

Influences

Researchers have pointed out that humans are social beings and rely on acquaintances. They are influenced by their acquaintances, perceptions of jobs and coworkers (Taylor, 1948), academia, timing (Fischer, 1996), evolution, progress, location, and many personal factors (Kerka, 1991).

Acquaintances at home, in school, and in the community influence many individuals' career decisions. People want to be accepted and fit in. Children are exposed to and influenced by parental attitudes, expectations, and professions, both positively and negatively. Parental views on gender roles, belief systems regarding gender, and actions toward both sexes inevitably influence children (Brown, 1999). Children are sent strong signals about the world around them, more specifically about men and women, from parents. Boitel (2002) stated that parents should examine their actions and words because they may be sending their children gender biased information about career opportunities. Hawkes and Brockmueller (2004) related this possibility directly to technology careers by stating that "the ubiquity of technology suggests that male/female differences in technology use may be shaped by parents" (p. 32).

Teachers and high school counselors also aid students in scripting their career itinerary to determine where they will go in life. In relating this influence to technology careers, Barker (1998) concluded that career counselors are often unfamiliar with careers and educational programs in mathematics, science and technology and do not advise students to enter those fields. Additionally, counselors sometimes base advisement on personal stereotypical beliefs and experiences. The National Women's Law Center (2000) discouraged this practice and insisted that "There should not be different counseling opportunities or admissions requirements based on whether you are male or female" (p. 5).

Barker (1998) said that by eliminating male-oriented projects in favor of a more gender-neutral curriculum, females might be encouraged to use technology more. Many respondents in Barker's study cited a need to educate guidance counselors who may consider technology education appropriate only for males or inappropriate for college-bound students (Barker, 1998).

Job characteristics, personal characteristics, and personal interests help define career choices. Brown (1999) stated that physical attributes, intelligence level, race, and gender are all precipitators of career and educational choices. Barker (1998) focused on job characteristics in career choices, claiming that job characteristics such as salary, working conditions, and co-workers also affect career decisions.

When career decisions are made is also important. Careers that are available, available training, and available space in training programs determine or open many possibilities for attending or not attending a training program or taking a job (CareerTech, 2005). Barker (1998) concluded that what is available combined with a multitude of other dynamics, create supply and demand for a profession and for students, and thus impact career decisions at any given time. He also added that where a person lives, where a company or business is located, and where training is located have an affect to either influence or, in some cases, create barriers discouraging choosing many occupations.

Barriers

Many barriers in career decisions exist because of ancient and pervasive beliefs that women lack reason and are emotional, which give males a dominant position in society. Reskin and Hartmann (1986) asserted that this belief underlies the social values that women are subordinate, stating that "Despite recent changes in attitudes and new

33

challenges to old beliefs, a variety of barriers—legal, institutional, and informal—still limit women's access to occupations in which men have customarily predominated" (p. 126). They concluded that it is difficult to change culture and in spite of all the effort in the past several years, there has been very little change in computer technology career participation.

Career education programs are a vital way to gain skills needed to obtain a job. The National Women's Law Center claimed, "some schools or programs may not give female students an equal opportunity to succeed in career education" (p. 3). The Center reported that barriers that females view as obstacles when selecting and entering non-traditional occupations include harassment, lack of role models, stereotype perceptions, and discrimination (National Women's Law Center, 2000).

Harassment in the classroom and on the job limits women in their career decisions. In *Workforce Education: Issues for the New Century* (Paulter, 1999), Susan Olson defined harassment as behavior that is excluding, demeaning, or intimidating. Harassment often occurs in schools, the workplace, and society at large. Males' chauvinistic attitudes toward females using computers in school or at work influence how females view technology, causing prejudices against technology. When boys tease girls about their lack of performance with technology and interest in games, they perpetuate those prejudices, provide an avenue for discrimination, and influence their choices to be or not to be computer scientist (Wakefield, 2004).

Herring (1999) talked about how males sometimes clearly harass, females causing them to either conform or retreat to themselves. According to Herring, gender harassment tends to be crude, direct, and sexually explicit by adolescents and post adolescents. When adult males question, criticize, and imply that females are incompetent with technology, they also influence female's decisions to enter technology careers. Herring pointed out that studies have indicated that in school and the workplace, sex bias has inhibited females from reaching their full potential in math, science and technology (1999).

However, some researchers have asserted that the scarcity of senior women role models has been the largest contributor to the failure of females to enter the field of technology. Boitel (2002) stated that "Having women in senior leadership roles in technology companies is critical to demonstrating to young women that such a career goal is feasible and desirable" (p. 2). As role models, female professionals might show girls the interesting and useful applications for technology, helping dispel the "geek" stereotypes that students might hold toward technology positions. Verbick (2002) felt that as more women complete computer science, engineering, and other technology degrees, new role models will be created and there will be an increase in the overall number of Information Technology professionals.

Lemons (2001) agreed that few female mentors have been available for girls when investigating technology career opportunities. According to Camp (2001), the most important move universities can make to improve this situation is to hire female faculty role models in computing departments, but this task may prove difficult with only 14-16 percent of the doctoral degrees awarded in computer science going to women. If, as suggested by some experts (e.g. Boitel, 2002; Camp, 2001; Verbick, 2002), the lack of strong female role models is the reason for the gender gap in technology use between males and females, it seems likely that girls who have witnessed other females in math, science and technology careers and developed communication with them may be more likely to seek technology degrees. These girls may perceive science and technology fields as acceptable careers for themselves.

Web sites aimed at providing information helping young women choose the computer science field have been successful in contributing to computer career equity through use of role models. The Role Model Project for girls (www.womenswork.org/girls /compsci/) encourages young girls to view random documents that contain information about women role models in computer science. The site allows young girls to study female role models and encourages women to post their own documents, becoming role models themselves. According to Verbick (2002), "Women just starting out in the computer science field all the way up to women who hold top positions at companies had posted their role model documents at this site" (p. 6).

According to some researchers, gender inequality in technology careers is also affected by the fact that computer scientists are portrayed or visualized in a way that implies they live and breathe technology. Brock (2002) reported that women are alienated by a stifling "geek culture" that celebrates obsessive computing at the expense of broad interests. In this cultural stereotype, the portrayed image has been that computer students and professionals work at the computer every waking moment and want to do nothing else. This image had been put forward as the expectation of a computer scientist. Image is important to adolescent girls, and some may have wondered why they should prepare for a career in technology if its image is viewed in a negative light. According to some researches, however, these expectations and norms are a form of prejudice and may not be accurate. "Stereotypes about appropriate and inappropriate occupations for women and men encourage sex-typical occupational choices by affecting workers' aspirations, self-image, identity, and commitment" (Reskin & Hartmann, 1986, p. 42). At a time when high-tech job opportunities are expanding, the literature indicates that many women are still socialized away from technology careers. Many females do not see the computer culture as people-friendly, let alone female-friendly, and thus cannot see themselves flourishing in such an environment. Larisa Kofman, president of the Women's Circle and a computer database editor, claimed that women's reluctance to pursue computer science majors relates to "a general fear of technology," whereas men become interested in technology and have more of a hands-on experience at a young age (Matthews, 1998).

An additional problem cited by some researchers is that counselors have been unfamiliar with careers and educational programs in mathematics, science and technology resulting from their own stereotypical beliefs. For example, Barker (1998) claimed that counselors have steered girls away from important mathematical prerequisites and industrial arts.

Equal opportunity supporters have been encouraging men and women to enter fields in which they have experienced discrimination. However, the number of women majoring in the computer sciences has not increased as it has in other fields such as legal and medical (Read, 2002). Some experts have claimed that boys' chauvinistic attitudes toward girls using computers in grade school, middle school and high school influence how females view technology, causing prejudices against technology. Discrimination has occurred in career counseling, classrooms, hiring practices, the workplace, and job promotion. "Sex discrimination occurs when you are treated differently just because you are female or because you are male" (National Women's Law Center, 2000, p. 4). Policies and practices such as applying different rules because you are pregnant,

requiring movement of heavy objects, and using a prejudiced test for admittance can also
be forms of discrimination (National Women's Law Center, 2000). "All counseling and
admissions requirements should treat males and females equally" (National Women's
Law Center, 2000, p. 5); however, bias from personal experiences influence counseling
advice. Researchers such as Barker (1998) and Read (2002) have stated that males and
females are not given the same advice and career counselors sometimes discourage girls
from entering non-traditional careers.

Another source of gender barriers in career decisions is early learning. Gilbert
(2002) suggested that from infancy through early childhood, girls received messages that
mathematics, science and technology were male domains. Strauss (1991) pointed to a
direct correlation between a child's early learning experiences and later achievement in
mathematics, science and technology, thus establishing a link between these early
messages and the later scholastic achievements that relate to career decisions and
barriers.

Some researchers have suggested an innate biological basis for technology career
barriers for women. At the National Bureau of Economic Research Conference on
Diversifying the Science & Engineering Workforce on January 14, 2005, Harvard
President Lawrence Summers (2005) addressed the issue of biological gender differences
and their effects on career choices. Summers listed three reasons why he thought there
was a gender difference. He said, "The first is what I call the high-powered job
hypothesis. The second is what I would call different availability of aptitude at the high
end, and the third is what I would call different socialization and patterns of
discrimination in a search" (¶ 2). While acknowledging "Nurture" issues in gender bias,

Summers also posited "Nature" issues. He stated that men and women are different and that those differences may be the reason that women are not as interested in science, math, and technology areas.

Gender Issues

Gender has played a part in labor division since caveman days. Reskin and Hartmann (1986) stated that "Beliefs about differences between the sexes, many of them taken as axiomatic, play an important role in the organization of social life" (p. 38). The pointed out that when a major concentration of one sex works in one area of employment, the labor market labels it sex segregation and that the overall percentage of sex segregation has been consistent since 1900 (Reskin & Hartmann, 1986). Hawkes and Brockmueller (2004) claimed that differences exist in computer use between males and females and students may retain these outlooks all through their schooling experience and into their careers, resulting in issues regarding the impact on students and sex segregation in training and careers. They stated that, "The idea that technology is a predominantly male activity is not only reinforced in the home, but children also assign gender differentiated roles to technology use based on their experience at school" (Hawkes & Brockmueller, 2004, p.32). One gender equity project looked at the causes of the imbalance. In this project, teachers talked about the gender issues they were seeing. They made efforts to recruit girls for their classes, but were unsuccessful and found that girls were reluctant to speak out about discrepancies in school experiences (Sanders & Nelson, 2004).

There is an informal organization for technical women in computing called "Systers" (Systers.com, 2005). This organization has over 2,800 Systers in 53 countries around the world. The main service is providing a private forum and database system to females. Members of Systers are females that are in the technology and provide support and encouragement to fellow Systers. The author participates in online discussions on the Systers web site regarding technological issues, gender bias, and discrimination in the male dominated world of technology. This forum allows females in technology fields to discuss and many times solve gender issues affecting them in their workplace.

In the area of vocational education, some researchers claim that females have been left behind (Strauss & et al, 1991). Vocational education has acquired a high tech glow in recent years, but a recent report by Cavanagh (2002) alleged that gender bias still pervaded the nation's high school vocational programs and that the U. S. Department of Education must help fix the problem. Theoretical approaches to career development have concentrated on problems that people experience as they choose, prepare for, enter, and adapt to work (Gray & Herr, 1998). Those problems include gender equity and the variance of their needs, interests, and experiences and are key elements in career decisions. Sanders and Nelson (2004) called for investigating continued gender bias in vocational theory and practice, asking for research to determine "What's going on that would lead to such gender disparities among students who sit in the same classrooms and learn from the same teachers?" (p. 75).

Despite calls for such research, some researchers continue to support innate gender differences such as those suggested by Summers (2005) and Reskin and Hartmann (1986). Gurian and Stevens (2004) claimed that "New brain imaging technologies confirm that genetically templated brain patterning by gender plays a far larger role than we realized" (p. 6). They reported that the female brain has a larger corpus callosum and hippocampus, stronger neural connectors in the temporal lobes, more serotonin, more oxytocin, more cortical areas for verbal and emotive functioning, and an active prefrontal cortex that develops at an earlier age which makes girls less impulsive. The male brain has more cortical areas dedicated to spatial-mechanical functioning, lateralized brain activity, operates with less blood flow, is structured to compartmentalize so multitasking is harder, and is set to renew, recharge, and reorient itself by entering what neurologists call a rest state (Gurian & Stevens, 2004).

Such research indicates differences based on gender in the human brain. Not only do we need to think about left brain/right brain dominance, we now need to look at female brain/male brain when determining what influences career decisions. There would perhaps be more females interested in technology careers if they realized that the main qualifications for were logic, process skills, critical thinking, and problem solving, (Computer Schools, 2004).

Technology usage has generally increased and has been embraced in homes, offices, and communities. Yet there are differences in the way that males and females interact with technology. Those differences generate inequitable personal, academic, and economic results (Hawkes & Brockmueller, 2004). Although changes for American women in family life, employment, and education have transpired since the beginning of the Women's Rights Movement in 1848, women are still considered a minority in diversity and equity statistics.

Federal Regulations and Equity

In 1923, Alice Paul, the leader of the National Woman's Party, drafted an Equal Rights Amendment for the United States Constitution, proposing that men and women

41

would have equal rights throughout the United States (Eisenberg & Ruthsdotter, 1998), but it was not until years later that Title VII of the 1964 Civil Rights Act was passed, prohibiting employment discrimination on the basis of sex as well as race, religion, and national origin. "When sex discrimination affects the 'terms or conditions of employment', it is illegal" (Equal Rights Advocates, 2003, ¶ 1). Those conditions include pay, job title, advancement, being hired or fired, and training opportunities (Equal Rights Advocates, 2003).

Women's Rights

Many overwhelming changes for American women regarding family life, religion, government, employment, and education have come about during the years following Paul's proposed Constitutional change. Progressive philosophies have supported social change and encouraged females to become active in politics to help promote social change. Progressive thinkers believe that everyone has unlimited potential that could be developed through education, and that democracy means that it is society's responsibility to provide an education for everyone, females included. However, "thirty years after the enactment of Title IX, the patterns of enrollment in vocational and technical programs look shockingly similar to the patterns that existed prior to passage of the law" (National Women's Law Center, 2002, p.3). The Center's investigations also discovered that females who enroll in a traditional female program "have fewer opportunities to take advanced level classes" (p. 5). One mission of workforce education is to provide career preparation for the disadvantaged, and women are listed as a group of the disadvantaged. However, according to Gray and Herr (1998), women still face glass ceilings and sticky floors because of their sex.

Federal legislation affecting career education is attempting to address this situation. The federal government funds the vocational programs in states and provides additional money for states that encourage male and female students to participate in non-traditional schooling. The Department of Education's Office of Vocational and Adult Education coordinates with federal agencies to guarantee programs such as career and technical education, the Workforce Investment Act (WIA), and Temporary Assistance for Needy Families (TANF) support the preparation of females for non-traditional careers (AAUW, 2005). The WIA of 1998 was designed to help workers transition into high-skill, high-wage jobs. Displaced homemakers, single parents, and students seeking nontraditional employment training were placed under the new WIA legislation (AAUW, 2005) to encourage their entry into improved career choices.

Technology jobs vary in salary depending on the position, but many technology careers are ranked in the top fifty paying jobs. Professional careers in technology areas can be very worthwhile for both men and women. Technology jobs provide economic opportunities but are normally focused toward a select few of mostly males. In addition to the high earning potential, technology careers can be both personally and professionally rewarding in that they are mentally stimulating and offer many opportunities for advancement (Verbick, 2002). Federal legislation is currently fostering access to these opportunities for females but research evidence suggests there is still room for improvement.

Recruitment of Females in Non-Traditional Careers

All students have the right to fair and equal treatment during recruitment without sex stereotypes or sex discrimination (National Women's Law Center, 2000). In 2001, the state of Oklahoma initiated a program called GirlTech. It was a career mentoring program utilizing e-mentoring. The pilot program had two sites that were located at the Meridian Technology Center in Stillwater and Francis Tuttle Technology Center in Oklahoma City. They increased the sites to three the next year and have added one or two sites each year. In 2006, they had eight sites. The program was started to attract and retain females to non-traditional careers, especially in areas involving math and science. This effect was prompted by the fact that the national percentage of females in technology, math, and science had decreased and Oklahoma was below the national average (CareerTech, 2004).

Many states had programs that were similar to what Oklahoma proponents envisioned, so Oklahoma representatives searched the Internet to identify model programs to assist in beginning a program in Oklahoma. They contacted people from Texas and Georgia vocational education offices in 2001 to gather information about their programs and found that the role of mentors was very important (CareerTech, 2002).

TechPrep (2004) published by Bristol Community College also supports a Web site for Women in Technology (WIT). The Web site states that the mission of the WIT program is to increase the numbers of women in technology. Therefore, women can pursue careers that provide the opportunity to make significant contributions, further their careers, improve the quality of life, and provide role models for younger women.

The Oklahoma CareerTech system began the e-mentoring program using the Internet as a mode of communication. Counselors, teachers, and site coordinators nominated female students who had an interest in the program, and each site selected 25 students to participate. The program has had problems in finding female mentors and in keeping the mentors in the program. However, there has been an increase in female participation and completion of secondary and postsecondary computer technology career clusters (CareerTech, 2006).

Universities such as Harvard, Massachusetts Institute of Technology (MIT), and Yale sponsor special programs for high school girls to attend summer classes in math, science, and technology. Harvard supports several programs to promote females in math, science, and technology. The Education with New Technologies (ENT); REACH and IMPACT; and Science, Technology, Engineering, and Math (STEM) are the three most popular programs in Massachusetts (umassp.edu, 2006). MIT has the MITe program for girls between their Junior and Senior years in high school. It is four-week summer residential school for 60 females to explore career decisions in an effort to recruit females to their technology programs (wtp.mit.edu, 2006). The Yale Herald (2005) reports that, Yale administration recognizes the fact and is making an effort to increase the number of females in technology.

Many corporations such as Hewlett Packard (2006), IBM (2001), Cisco (2006), and Microsoft (2005) also support and have special incentives and programs for females. Cisco's website first frequently questioned why don't girls sign up is answered by stating that recruitment of females has to be proactive to overcome the strong negative messages that girls receive (Ciscolearning.org, 2006). IBM (2001) claims to be among the leaders in the field of technology and in their commitment to women, stating that "Founder T. J. Watson recruited women for top positions and promised equal pay for the same kind of work – three decades before the Equal Pay Act mandated other companies to do the same" (¶ 2).

Association of Women Scientists, National Scientists Fund, and Girl Scouts are among a host of groups that offer encouragement to females inquiring about non-traditional opportunities (Barker, 1998). Spain, New Zealand, United Kingdom, Australia, and other countries also have encouraged females to participate in non-traditional careers. There are web sites such as Systers.org, NetWomen.ca, and WIT.org that promote awareness and mentoring for females in technology. Much has been done, but the problem persists. More needs to be done in Oklahoma, across America, and globally to realize constant and systemic change (CareerTech, 2006) in the participation of females in the field of technology.

Summary of Literature Review

Computer technology careers are relatively new professions in comparison to farming, teaching, ranching, and manufacturing. Computing skills are used in many professions and new computer technology careers evolve from continued technology innovations.

Career choice models originated or developed with the addition of vocational education to the traditional liberal arts style of education. Models for career selection were used to assist students match interest and ability to career choices in an effort to guide educational pathways. Career models have been used in many ways and many areas of education. Oklahoma CareerTechs use career models to assist students in placement. Career selections are affected by various and numerous forces. Those influences and barriers limit, enhance, and determine decisions about work professions.

Some professions are dominated by gender. Computer technology has been dominated by males since conception. Efforts to recruit females in computer technology professions have not increased the percentage of females working in computer technology fields. Computer technology professions provide opportunities for job advancement, salary enhancement, and personal satisfaction that may not be available to females if barriers prevent females from choosing computer technology professions.

CHAPTER III

METHODOLOGY

General Approach

This study was descriptive in nature and used the survey method to collect data.

"Descriptive statistics provide a picture of what happened in the study" (Shavelson, 1996,

p. 8), by using a collection of conceptions and techniques employed in organizing,

analyzing, tabulating, and describing the data. The survey method gives a numeric

account of answers from a sample or population (Creswell, 2003). The three major

characteristics of surveys are that the information is collected to describe a population, is

usually obtained from a sample rather than the entire population, and that the information

is collected through asking questions. Questionnaires are the most common type of

instrument used in survey research (Fraenel & Wallen, 2003).

This study's online questionnaire gathered information from student responses to

conduct a descriptive study. The responses to the questionnaire were submitted

anonymously from the web site to a data base and were compiled to analyze input about

influences and barriers affecting career decisions. Students were identified as computer

technology majors or non-technology majors depending on the CareerTech program they

attended. Demographical profiles were constructed and compared. Responses were then

divided by gender and analyzed for comparison.

Population

The population for the study was adult students in Oklahoma that were attending a CareerTech Center. The Oklahoma CareerTech students were selected as the population because of potential access to students that have made career choices and have opportunities to pursue a program in a computer technology field. The students were 18 years of age or older and currently enrolled at one of the 29 Oklahoma Career and Technology Centers located at 55 different campuses throughout the state. The CareerTech campuses provided access to an ample number of participants to produce a valuable and worthwhile study. There were approximately 13,000 students in the target population over the age of 18 attending classes at the Oklahoma CareerTech Centers. Because of the methodological procedures used, not all of the targeted population received the information about the survey, thus it is not possible to determine the actual available population size that had opportunity to complete the survey.

Students that did participate may have been biased about technology because of experience with technology, thus skewing the results. The obtained results were not representative of the population if students that were uncomfortable with technology do not participate. "The external validity of a research study is the extent to which the findings of a particular study can be generalized to people or situations other than those observed in the study" (Shavelson, 1996). This represented a limitation of the study and suggested that caution was appropriate in generalizing its findings beyond the sample.

Sample

"Both design and execution of sampling can affect validity of the research. Design is how you choose the sample. Execution is how you obtain the data from the sample" (Henry, 1990, p. 13). The ability of a researcher to extend findings beyond the sample is referred to as generalization (Creswell, 2003; Henry, 1990). Threats to external validity occurs when inaccurate inferences are generalized beyond the sample group to other persons, settings, and situations (Creswell, 2003). "The extent to which the results of a study can be generalized determines the external validity of the study" (Fraenkel & Wallen, 2003, p. 109).

Since the sample size directly affects the sampling variability, there is almost always a concern about obtaining a sample that is large enough for statistical purposes. "Efficient sample size calculations are ways to estimate the size of the sample needed to fulfill the study objectives once a particular selection technique has been chosen" (Henry, 1990, p. 53). Rarely can a researcher collect data from all the subjects of interest in a particular study, but a small sample threatens the validity because of limitations to variability, however the larger sample size decreases the variance by reducing the size of the outliers, thus improving validity (Henry, 1990).

The data should come from all the people who can contribute information (Evensen, 2005). "The sample size is the most potent method of achieving estimates that are sufficiently precise and reliable" (Henry, 1990, p. 117). The researcher should be aware of the risks posed to external validity by the sample size (Henry, 1990). The sample size can be critical to avoid false conclusions and larger sample sizes can compensate or reduce variation (Henry, 1990). Self-selection threatens the sample size and places limitations on the ability in obtaining a large sample. Self-selection also effects who participates. In spite of the many benefits associated with Internet surveys, recent studies have identified a number of important limitations to Internet-based survey research. Even though the Internet has evolved to be a major information pipeline and is used by the general public, not all students are comfortable or competent with the Internet and may not participate because of having to use the Internet (Evensen, 2005). It was not possible to determine the effects of Internet survey deployment on this study's obtained sample.

There were 512 responses submitted. Fifty-five of the responses were incomplete and were removed from the study. Twenty-three of the responses came from students under the age of 18 and were eliminated. Ten of the responses were unusable because of inaccurate information such as a program that does not exist or listed the center instead of the program. Therefore the sample for this study consisted of 424 usable responses. This was deemed by the researcher as adequate for a valid descriptive study.

Of the 55 Oklahoma campuses, 19 (35%) campuses participated with at least one student completing and submitting the online questionnaire. The number of students from each participating campus is listed in Table 2. The total number of participants in the sample was 424.

Table 2

CareerTech Campuses Participating in the Study and Number of Participating Students from Each Campus

CareerTech Campus (Location)	Number of Participating Students (N=424) (n)
Mid-America (Wayne)	100
Northwest (Alva)	65
Caddo-Kiowa (Ft. Cobb)	41
Kiamichi (Durant)	40

Kiamichi (Hugo)	37
High Plains (Woodward)	28
Kiamichi (Talihina)	25
Kiamichi (Stigler)	15
Kiamichi (Atoka)	14
Green Country (Okmulgee)	13
Canadian Valley (Chickasha)	11
Metro Tech-South Bryant (Oklahoma City)	9
Northeast East (Kansas)	9
Metro Tech-Springlake (Oklahoma City)	8
Indian Capital-Bill Willis (Tahlequah)	3
Kiamichi (Poteau)	2
Southern Oklahoma (Ardmore)	2
Gordon Cooper (Shawnee)	1
Kiamichi (McAlester)	1

Note: Total for Kiamichi was 234.
Note: Total for Oklahoma City was 17.

According to the Oklahoma CareerTech definition, there are two metro areas

(Tulsa and Oklahoma City) with six campuses and 49 campuses in rural locations

(CareerTech, 2004). In the sample for this study, there were two of the six metro

campuses (33%) and 17 of the 49 rural campuses (35%).

Instrumentation

"A survey design provides a quantitative or numeric description of trends,

attitudes, or opinions of a population" (Creswell, 2003, p. 153), however, "the problem to be investigated by means of a questionnaire should be sufficiently interesting and important enough to motivate the individuals surveyed to respond" (Fraenkel & Weller, 2003, p. 398). A survey can be used to maximize the sample in a minimum length of time for the least amount of expense and uses modern technology to help provide anonymity and a sufficient sample size. Therefore, despite limitations presented above, an online survey was selected as the method to collect data for this study. The Internet was used because it permitted the researcher to potentially reach all of the students in the Oklahoma CareerTech system without restrictions due to geographic location. It saved money by not having to print the questionnaire and saved researcher time by having the questionnaire submitted directly to the server. The information submitted by participants was automatically saved to an Excel file instead of a person physically inputting the data, which also saved time and money.

The proper steps and references were made to insure reliability and validity of the study's questionnaire. Validity refers to whether the questionnaire measured what it intended to measure. "The validity of a questionnaire relies first and foremost on reliability" (Evensen, 2005, ¶ 1). "Reliability is a characteristic of the instrument itself, but validity comes from the way the instrument is employed" (¶ 3). The method used to gather the data should match the information needed to make assumptions about the data.

The instrument and understanding the questions on the instrument are threats that should be addressed to increase internal validity (Fraenkel & Wallen, 2003). For this study, self-reporting and the clarity of the question were the most serious threats to internal validity. By allowing participants to self-report, the results were more reliant on the honesty and understanding of the respondent (GVU, 1998). This limitation was unavoidable and accepted as a potential source of bias in this study. "Improperly worded questions can only result in biased or otherwise meaningless responses" (Kidder & Judd, 1986, p. 243). Several steps, discussed below, were taken to address this issue.

Survey length can be a problem that is universally recognized by researchers (Henry, 1990). The length of a survey can limit the participation of potential respondents because of the length of time involved in survey response. This problem was addressed in this study by keeping the questionnaire short, so it was not time-consuming and took only approximately fifteen minutes to complete.

Another known problem with self-selection has been that the respondents might take the survey more than once (Henry, 1990). There was no way to know if students took the questionnaire in this study more than once because of submitting anonymously, thus making the assumption of the uniqueness of each of the 424 participants a limitation of this study.

The problems with self-reporting were addressed by making the introduction to the survey, consent form, and questionnaire as brief and through as possible. Any ambiguity in reading the instructions and consent form was reduced as much as possible by creating a simple web site. The web site was blue and red, with large font sizes for ease of reading and use. In addition, the questionnaire was user friendly and easy to administer with limited choices. The questions were presented in a manner that was easy to understand, and the content was relevant to the life experiences of all who might respond to the questionnaire. The purpose of the study was briefly stated on the web page and allowed them to choose to either exit the questionnaire or to become a participant. It also stated on the introduction web page that participants should be honest in their responses.

The questionnaire was straight forward and there was no known reason for the respondents to misrepresent themselves or their responses. Questions from previously used questionnaires were incorporated into the present instrument and additional questions that are clear and concise were added. The questions were worded as to not to elicit a particular response or mislead participants.

The questionnaire was spaced so that participants could see which question and which response was being selected to eliminate selection errors. All questions were analyzed by the researcher for clarity, ambiguity, and validity. The reading level of each question was checked and each question was analyzed for sensitive wording. Since the questionnaire was designed to permit students freedom to take the questionnaire at their convenience, there was a possibility of taking the questionnaire with other students and it was possible that participants may have been influenced by others that were taking the questionnaire at the same time.

Outside opinion and critiques were solicited from the researcher's colleagues to eliminate possibilities of questions being personal, inappropriate, or offensive. The questionnaire was easy to access on the Internet and easy to complete. The 55 campuses of Oklahoma CareerTech all have computers available for students to use at all hours of the day and night. The questionnaire was available for student participation for several weeks over a two month period.

"It is important to pretest the questions to revise and improve them" (Kidder & Judd, 1986, p. 243), so the questionnaire was reviewed in a college technology class to evaluate the questions for understanding and relevance. The college students made comments about each question on the questionnaire and from those comments, questions were selected to be included as part of the questionnaire.

The questionnaire was then piloted with another group of students for interpretation, and corrections and additions were made to the questionnaire. Next the dissertation committee made suggestions and made additional corrections. The questionnaire was shared with colleagues and advice and input was received from them to clarify each question in each section to establish content validity.

After extensive research, collaborative discussion, and constructive critiques, it was determined that the design and construction of the survey instrument was valid and would produce reliable results. Every precaution known to the researcher was used to insure as few problems as possible, and it is believed that the research yielded results that will have value in the recruitment of non-traditional students to the technology field.

Instructors did not have to use class time to administer the questionnaire because the questionnaire was available online at any time of the day. The questionnaire was available for participants to take during their leisure time. It released instructors from responsibility to administer the questionnaire, collect the questionnaires, and return them to the researcher. Questionnaires administered "live" on a single day decrease the opportunity for students to participate in the study because of absences (Evensen, 2005). In contrast, online availability over a period of time allows them the opportunity to participate instead of losing the opportunity because of being absent the day the questionnaire was administered at the school. Thus, the researcher believes that putting the questionnaire online increased the chance of students being aware of the study and choosing to become a participant, thus increasing the return rate of the questionnaire and the representativeness of the sample.

The online questionnaire costs for the domain name and the monthly hosting fees were minimal. There was no mailing charge, cost for printing, storage, or housing of equipment. Additionally, there was no travel expense or telephone charges because of cell phone usage.

The questionnaire (Appendix A) contained 60 questions and was divided into three sections. Each section was clearly identified and students could exit the survey at any time.

The first section of the questionnaire gathered demographic information in questions one through 16. The format of those 16 questions was designed from a model made available by Graphics, Visualization, & Usability Center on their website (http://www.gvu.gatech.edu/user_surveys/survey-1998-10/graphs/general/q54.htm), the United States Census, and other examples. Seven of the questions were general demographic questions about gender, age, race, grade classification, residence area, income, and marital status. The other nine questions asked for specific information about counseling assistance, campus location, specific program of CareerTech, and parental involvement in technology.

The second section was comprised of 24 statements numbered 17 through 40 which collected responses to items related to career decisions regarding exposure to computers, external factors, and personal perceptions about computers. Questions 17 through 28 asked specific questions about parents; siblings; and use of computers, cell phones, and technology games. The responses were recorded using a five-point Likert scale, with five (5) being "Very Often" and one (1) being "Never". Questions numbered 29 through 40 utilized statements from a survey and interview questions used by Stansell and Starkweather (2004) to conduct research about females majoring in technology at a regional university in Oklahoma. The responses were recorded using a five-point Likert scale, with five (5) being "Strongly agree" and one (1) being "Strongly disagree".

The third section measured influences on career and educational choices shaped by contact and exposure to certain individuals during a student's life. Section three used a six-point Likert scale measuring five (5) degrees of positive or negative influences and a sixth choice of not-applicable. Items 41 through 60 were derived from items on a survey used by Flowers (2001). The survey was "in accordance with the requirements of the Office of Gender Equity for Career Development, Virginia Department of Education, the Carl Perkins Act, and other federal and state laws and regulations" (Flowers, 2001, p. 45). Flowers' study was supported by the U.S. Department of Education. Flowers has spent more than 15 years studying female enrollment in technology education identifying obstacles to women in selecting technology education as a career (Barker, 1998). This section identified positive and negative influences which were represented by numerical values of five (5) for very positive, Four (4) for somewhat positive, three (3) for neutral, two (2) for somewhat negative, one (1) for negative, and zero (0) representing not applicable.

The responses to the questionnaire yielded tabulatable data information used for descriptive analysis that included frequencies, percentages, and cross-tabulation.

Procedures

Oklahoma State University IRB approval (Appendix B) was obtained on December 10, 2005, before the online questionnaire was uploaded on the Internet. Accompanying the online questionnaire were instructions asking respondents to answer the questions on their own, honestly, and to the best of their ability. The consent form (Appendix C) was constructed as a webpage and contained the only link to the online questionnaire. Access to answer the questionnaire was contingent on the student's consent and all data were submitted anonymously.

This questionnaire for the study was administered online, but was not a typical online survey where the participants see the survey online at a popular web site or receive an e-mail advising them of the availability of the survey. Some 9.5 million Americans now use the Internet, including 8.4 million adults and 1.1 million children under 18, who tap into it from the workplace, school and homes. Obviously, the study did not wish to have inappropriate participation from this huge and largely irrelevant population. To specifically reach only the CareerTech student population of interest, a list of e-mail addresses of a contact person at each CareerTech campus was provided by the state CareerTech Guidance Coordinator. An e-mail was then sent to each of the 55 campuses recruiting their support in providing information to the CareerTech students and providing an opportunity for students to contribute to the study. A website was created to distribute the questionnaire. The website address was available to all CareerTech students, but the study focused only on those 18 years of age or older. There was nothing to prevent students that were younger than 18 from taking the questionnaire, and there

59

were in fact 23 students aged 16 or 17 years old who submitted responses. These were removed from the usable data.

There was no direct interaction by the researcher with participants or teachers. A representative from the state CareerTech office suggested that the Campus Directors be the contact person. An e-mail address for each Campus Director was supplied to the researcher by the CareerTech administrative office. There was initially limited participation from students with Directors dispersing procedures to participate. One Campus Director suggested that the Education Enhancement Coordinator on each campus disperse information about the survey to the students. Upon that advice, the Education Enhancement Coordinators (EECs) were contacted and provided with information to share with students.

Support from CareerTech administrators and Campus Directors in administering the questionnaire was very beneficial. Their assistance proved to be crucial in gathering an adequate number of participants. There were no incentives for participation other than topical interest. Oklahoma CareerTech encourages and promotes student entrance into non-traditional courses of study. The CareerTech administration was therefore keenly interested in developing participation in this study in order to have access to the data and results generated for the study. Therefore, CareerTech administration encouraged all Campus Directors to encourage all instructors to encourage all students to participate in the online questionnaire, thus substantially increasing the probability of student participation. The study methodology did require Directors to forward the introductory survey information to their instructors and did require the instructors to advise students as to the availability of the questionnaire, administrative interest in student participation, interest in the survey results, and the online survey location. Campus Directors were contacted via e-mail and asked to encourage students to participate and maintain the support of administrators and instructors. After the Campus Directors elicited the assistance of their EECs, 33% of the CareerTech campuses had students participate in the study.

The questionnaire was made available online to students for two months, December and January, during the 2005-2006 school year. Two follow up e-mails to Education Enhancement Coordinators were sent asking to make information about the survey available for students. When all data had been obtained, they were compiled and analyzed via the SPSS computer program.

Analysis of the Data

The five research questions that guided this study were addressed using descriptive statistics. A general descriptive profile of the sample was developed from the responses of the first 16 survey questions that were identified as a demographical section of the survey.

The first research question, "What is the demographic profile of students who pursue careers in computer technology and how does it compare with non-technology career clusters?", also used the first 16 survey questions to construct a profile for computer technology students and non-technology students based on frequencies and percentages.

The second research question, "Are those demographic profiles the same for males and females?" utilized responses from demographic questions one through 16 to compare males and females. The responses of females and males in computer technology

61

programs were compared and analyzed and responses of females and males in non-technology programs were compared and analyzed.

The third research question, "What is the profile of influences and barriers for students who pursue careers in computer technology and how does it compare with non-technology career clusters?", utilized responses from survey questions 17-60.

The fourth research question, "Are those influences the same for male and female students?", utilized responses from those same survey questions used to analyze the third research question. The responses of females and males in computer technology programs were compared and analyzed and responses of females and males in non-technology programs were compared and analyzed.

The fifth research question compared logically and conceptually a career model developed from this study to existing career choice models. Moody's Model is gender-specific and identifies influences and barriers that are significant in the selection of computer technology careers at Oklahoma CareerTechs.

CHAPTER IV

FINDINGS

Demographics Profile for the General Sample

Demographics provide general information about a group. General demographic

information about people includes such characteristics as age, education, income, and

gender. Demographics provide valuable information about the sample and can be

compared to population demographics to check for fair representation (Kohl, 2004).

This study utilized demographic information for extended details about the

participants. The responses were used to identify patterns, frequencies, and groups. There

were 16 survey questions in the demographic section of the survey. Seven general

questions included: age, gender, income, residence, ethnicity, marital status, and grade

level and there were nine specific demographic questions about the campus, program,

program selection process, program availability, disabilities, career counseling, and

parental computer work experience. Survey question number seven, identifying the

specific training program in which subjects were enrolled, was used to determine if

students were in a Computer Technology (CT) program or a Non-Technology (NT)

program. Computer technology programs were defined in this study as Career Cluster

programs that focused on computer skills. They included: Arts, A/V Technology and

Communications; Business, Management & Administration; Information Technology;

and Science, Technology, Engineering, and Mathematics. Non-technology programs were defined as Career Cluster programs that did not focus on computer skills. They included: Agriculture, Food, & Natural Resources; Architecture & Construction; Education & Training; Finance; Government & Public Administration; Health Science; Hospitality & Tourism; Human Services; Law, Public Safety & Security; Manufacturing; Marketing, Sales & Service; and Transportation, Distribution & Logistics.

Of the 424 usable responses, 173 (40.8%) were identified as participating in a CT career cluster as defined above. One hundred thirty-five of the 173 responses listed business CT, business and information technology, or some combination of those terms to indicate that they were participating in a CT program. Sixteen listed computer repair and networking, 17 listed web design, four listed E-commerce and technology, and one listed video production/multimedia as the program that they were currently attending.

There were 251 (59.2%) students majoring in a NT program such as auto collision, carpentry, horticulture, law enforcement, welding, culinary arts, health care, and education. Auto technology and diesel technology were also identified as NT programs even though the term technology was used and computers were used in diagnosing problems. The accounting, nursing, manufacturing, and medical transcription programs also use computers and students received extensive training on computers but were not identified as CT careers as defined in this study. A representative from the Oklahoma CareerTech assisted in analyzing student responses and determining if the program was in one of the CT career clusters or not.

Of the 424 usable student responses, 199 (46.9%) were males and 225 (53.1%) were females. This was close to an equal distribution by gender.

Age distribution reflected what age group was attending the CareerTech programs. Technical schools were developed to assist young students gain skills to become employed, but have broadened their student profiles through the years. The ages of the students that participated in this study ranged from 18 to 88. A complete distribution of individual ages was listed in Table 3.

Table 3

Ages, Frequencies, and Percentages of Sample (N=424)

Ages	Frequencies	Sample Percentages[a]
18	204	48.1%
19	43	10.1%
20	17	4.0%
21	17	4.0%
22	0	0.0%
23	10	2.4%
24	12	2.8%
25	5	1.2%
26	1	0.2%
27	5	1.2%
28	3	0.7%
29	4	0.9%
30	12	2.8%
31	5	1.2%
32	5	1.2%
33	3	0.7%
34	4	0.9%
35	5	1.2%
36	2	0.5%
37	1	0.2%
38	4	0.9%
39	3	0.7%
40	2	0.5%
41	3	0.7%
42	3	0.7%
43	6	1.4%
44	2	0.5%
45	5	1.2%
46	3	0.7%
47	3	0.7%
48	4	0.9%

49	9	2.1%
50	2	0.5%
51	2	0.5%
52	1	0.2%
53	1	0.2%
54	1	0.2%
55	2	0.5%
56	3	0.7%
57	1	0.2%
58	4	0.9%
59	0	0.0%
60	1	0.2%
61-87	0	0.0%
88	1	0.2%

[a]Rounding errors may have prevented percentages from equaling 100%.

Two hundred four (48.1%) were 18 years of age and 43 (10.1%) were 19 years of age. The 18 and 19 year old students were combined to form a group of students under twenty and students that were 20-29 were grouped together, as were students in the thirties, forties, and fifties. There were only two students sixty and older, so they were grouped together. The grouped age distribution is shown in Table 4.

Table 4

Grouped Ages, Frequencies, and Percentages of Sample (N=424)

Grouped Ages	Frequencies	Sample Percentages [a]
18-19	247	58.3%
20-29	74	17.5%
30-39	44	10.4%
40-49	40	9.4%
50-59	17	4.0%
60-88	2	0.5%

[a]Rounding errors may have prevented percentages from equaling 100%.

The ages were grouped to reduce the number of age groups and eliminate groups of one or two. This provided a clear picture of the ages represented in the sample. The sample was generally young, with approximately three-quarters (75.8%) under the age of 30, and more than one-half (58.3%) under the age of 20.

The term race or ethnicity distinguishes one population of humans from another and categories are often based on visible traits (race.eserver.org, 2006). Caucasian/White is a generic category for many nationalities such as German, Russian, Canadian, and American, because of the skin color. Asians, Africans, and Native Americans are also identified because of physical traits rather than birth location. Asians are not necessarily from Asia and Africans are not always from Africa. Native Americans have many tribes comprising the category. Hispanic and Latino also are comprised of several countries or groups of people. The sample frequency distribution and sample percentages by ethnicity are listed in Table 5.

Table 5

Ethnicity, Frequencies, and Percentages of Sample (N=424)

Ethnicity	Frequencies	Sample Percentages [a]
Caucasian/White	288	67.9%
African American	23	5.4%
Native American	75	17.6%
Asian	1	0.2%
Hispanic	21	4.9%
Latino	3	0.7%
Multiracial	9	2.1%
Other	4	0.9%

[a]Rounding errors may have prevented percentages from equaling 100%.

The table was constructed using responses from students who were required to select, through self-identification, their ethnicity. There was a category labeled "Other" with a comment section, and four students responded by identifying themselves as "Other". There was one with no comment. There were three with comments of clarification that reported "German /Russian", "Hispanic/White", and "Indian, Mexican". Those four that selected "Other" were counted in the "Other" category, even though the "German/Russian" could have been classified Caucasian/White while the

"Hispanic/White" and "Indian, Mexican" could have been classified as multiracial. There were four that selected an ethnic race, but added a comment or qualifier. One selected Native American, but added the comment "and some white." That student was counted in the Native American category. Three students selected Caucasian/White, but one added the comment, German. Another listed Native American in comment section and the third student added n/a to the comment section. The eighth did not select an ethnic choice, but added white in the comment section. The three that selected Caucasian/White and the one that did not select a choice but added the comment, "white" were counted in the Caucasian/White category. The sample was generally Caucasian with almost 70%.

The current grade level of participating students was Junior 104 (24.5%), Senior 100 (23.5%), Post-secondary 158 (37.2%), and Other 62 (14.6%). There were 204 (48.1%) High School Juniors and Seniors, and 220 (51.9%) in Post-secondary and "Other" category which was about half. Postsecondary students attend a wide variety of academic and vocational programs beyond the high school level that may lead to a degree or to improvement in one's knowledge or career skills. The 62 subjects that responded "Other" consisted of 15 that listed adult, eight that listed Vo-tech or technical student, eight listed a "two-year tech program", and one listed a "one-year tech program". Six listed first year, four listed that they had two years of college, one listed tenth grade, one listed second year student, one self identified as a college Junior, one as a college Senior, one as graduated, one as having a Master's Degree, one listed 13 as the grade level, and one marked "Other" and filled in "n/a". One listed "Freshman", but did not indicate high school or college. Four listed two years of college. Seven other listings were 1) "high school grad", 2) "just started", 3) "Technology Education", 4) "out of school", 5) "first

68

time student", 6) "Advanced Accounting", and 7) "past high school". There were more

Post-secondary students than high school students in the sample. The Post-secondary and

"Other" categories combined constituted a group of adults, no longer in high school,

while the Juniors and Seniors constituted a group of students still in high school,

indicating a nearly equal division of the sample.

Survey question number nine was designed to identify if the students were from

urban or rural areas. The metro campuses had very few participants, so it was difficult to

compare urban and rural responses. Two hundred forty-one (56.8%) of the total sample

were from a town and 153 (36.1%) were from a rural area, which totaled 394 (92.9%) of

the sample. Suburban and urban areas had fifteen (3.5%) participants each, which

represented only 7.1% of the sample. Thus, the sample was nearly completely non-urban

in nature. Urban was defined as Oklahoma City or Tulsa on the survey. Suburban was

defined as a residential region near a major city. Town and rural were not defined on the

survey.

The survey categorized family income into ten categories. The majority of the

students, 181 (42.7%), reported family income of under $10,000. There were 15 (3.5%)

students that reported their family income as $90,000 and over. The complete breakdown

of all ten categories was listed in Table 6.

Table 6

Family Income, Frequencies, and Percentages of Sample (N=424)

Family Income	Frequencies	Sample Percentages
0 - $9,999	181	42.7%
$10,000-$19,999	45	10.6%
$20,000-$29,999	41	9.7%
$30,000-$39,999	42	9.9%
$40,000-$49,999	40	9.4%

69

$50,000-$59,999	23	5.4%
$60,000-$69,999	16	3.8%
$70,000-$79,999	14	3.3%
$80,000-$89,999	7	1.7%
≥$90,000	15	3.5%

There was a decrease in the number of students in each of the higher income brackets until the bracket of "$90,000 and Over." The sample was generally students primarily in the lower income brackets.

The marital status results showed that 300 (70.8%) were single, 65 (15.3%) were married, 39 (9.2%) divorced, 14 (3.3%) separated, and six (1.4%) widowed. The sample was largely single students.

Survey question 12 of the demographic section asked about the number of siblings at home. One hundred forty-five (34.2%) of the students had no siblings at home. One hundred twenty-four (29.2%) had one sibling, 86 (20.3%) had two siblings at home, 42 (9.9%) had three siblings at home, and 27 (6.4%) had four or more siblings at home. Most students had no siblings at home, but a large portion had one sibling at home.

Survey questions number 13 and 14 questioned if a parent was working in the technology field. In response to whether fathers worked in the technology field, there were 15 (3.5%) that responded yes, 388 (91.5%) reported no, and 21 (5.0%) were not sure; whereas if mothers were working in the technology field the responses were 56 (13.2%) yes, 353 (83.3%) were no, and 15 (3.5%) were not sure as reported in Table 7.

Table 7

Parents Working in a Technology Field Frequencies and Percentages of Sample (N=424)

Parents in Technology	Father Frequencies & Percentages	Mother Frequencies & Percentages
Yes	15 (3.5%)	56 (13.2%)
No	388 (91.5%)	353 (83.3%
Not Sure	21 (5.0%)	15 (3.5%)

Exposure and opportunity play a part in career choices. Existing career models have indicated that parental jobs sometimes influence children's career choices as children follow in parental footprints. However, the vast majority of students in this sample reported that neither parent worked in a technology field, regardless of their own career training choice. Among the students who reported that one of their parents did work in a technology field, more than three times as many had mothers working in a technology position than fathers. Twenty-one students were not sure if their father worked in a technology field and 15 students were not sure if their mother worked in a technology field.

Aptitude and interest tests have been used by school teachers and counselors to help students determine a career path. Survey question number five was designed to determine if students had special guidance in career selection. The data showed that there were 37 (8.8%) with Temporary Assistance for Needy Families (TANF), six (1.4%) listed as Displaced Homemakers, two (0.5%) in the Dropout Recovery Program, 24 (5.7%) listed as Other, and 355 (83.7%) reported None. Students were provided a section for comments to clarify "Other." The comments in the comment section were: Rehab, workforce, military, Education Enhancement Center, ASCOG (Association of South Central Oklahoma Government) Displaced Worker, anger management, welding training,

71

and continuing education, and all the help I can get. One participant marked "Other" and then the comment was "n/a". The majority (83.7%) of the students did not appear to have received school guidance in choosing a career field.

During recruitment and enrollment, students select which CareerTech program they would like to attend. Some programs have restrictions and requirements such as a limited number of students at a given time or prerequisites. Survey question number seven asked if the program that they were currently attending was their first choice. Three hundred seventy-eight (89.2%) students were admitted into the program of their first choice. Forty-six (10.8%) were not admitted into their first choice. Nineteen of the 46 who reported that they were not admitted into their first choice failed to comment or give explanation. Twenty-seven of the 46 identified the program that was their first choice. Five listed LPN, four listed health science, two listed cosmetology, one each listed nursing, auto paint and body, machine tool, medical technician, diesel mechanic, radio broadcasting, wood shop, auto tech, aviation maintenance/engineering, heat and air, medical billing/coding, and welding. One student reported that they originally had enrolled in medical administration but that they did not like medical administration, so they changed to general accounting. Another student said they transferred to web design, but did not list what program they originally began. One wanted law instead of welding. One said that welding was the first choice but was blind in their left eye and could not do the program. These data suggested that while some CareerTech students were not participating in their first choice career program, the large majority (89.2%) gained access to the career field training they preferred.

Some CareerTech programs have prerequisites or a selection process. Of the 424 participants, there was a selection process for 66 (15.6%) and not for 358 (84.4%) of the students. There were 21 responses on the comment section, which indicated that 15 had to interview, three took a placement test, one said if they had available space, one response was TABE SAGE (Test of Adult Basic Education, and System for Assessment and Group Evaluation), and one checked that they had requirements but did not list the requirements. These data suggested that for most CareerTech students (84.4%) access to career training was not constrained by prerequisites or selection processes.

Survey question number 16 was designed to identify learning disabilities, including physical, economical, and mental. Disability categories included visually impaired; hearing impaired; motor development; cognitively disadvantaged; academically disadvantaged; or economically disadvantaged. These categories are identified and defined by the CareerTech system.

Students could list as many disabilities that applied to them. Three hundred twenty-one (75.7%) did not list a disability or disadvantage. Of the 103 (24.3%) students that listed at least one disability or disadvantage, 17 listed two disabilities, three listed three disabilities, one listed five disabilities and one listed all six disabilities or disadvantages.

Of the 17 students that listed two disabilities, one listed vision and academically disadvantaged; one student listed vision and economically disadvantaged; one listed cognitively disadvantaged and economically disadvantaged; one listed hearing and economically disadvantaged; one listed impaired motor development and academically disadvantaged; two listed vision and hearing; two listed hearing and academically disadvantaged; two listed motor development and economically disadvantaged; and six

listed academically disadvantaged and economically disadvantaged.

Of the three students that listed three disabilities, one listed motor development,

cognitively disadvantaged, and economically disadvantaged; and two listed vision,

hearing, and economically disadvantaged. One listed five disabilities including hearing,

motor development, cognitively disadvantaged, academically disadvantaged, and

economically disadvantaged but not vision. One student selected all six disabilities. Table

8 displays the disabilities selected.

Table 8

Disabilities, Frequencies, and Percentages of Sample (N=424)

Disabilities[a]	Frequencies	Percentages[b]
Vision	33	7.8%
Hearing	18	4.2%
Motor Development	11	2.6%
Cognitively Disadvantaged	6	1.4%
Academically Disadvantaged	29	6.8%
Economically Disadvantaged	38	9.0%

[a]Students could select more than one disability.
[b]Rounding errors may have prevented percentages from equaling 100%.

Of the disabilities listed, economically disadvantaged was listed most often,

vision was the next highest, and academically disadvantaged was the third highest. There

were 135 disabilities reported from 103 students.

These data suggested that the majority of the CareerTech students (75%) believed

they had no disabilities or disadvantages. Only a very small group (n=22 or 0.05%) had

multiple disabilities.

Summary of Demographics Profile for the General Sample

The sample consisted mostly (58.2%) of young, 18-19 years old, students that were single (70.8%), Caucasian (67.9%), with family incomes of less than $10,000 (42.7%), and living in small towns (56.8%) or rural areas (36.1%). The sample was almost equally divided between males and females and between students in high school and post-secondary students.

Most (83.7%) received no career guidance or counseling at the CareerTech campuses. There were no career program selection processes for 84.4%, and 89.2% were admitted in the program of choice. Most students (n=335 or 79%) had neither parent working in a technology field, but a larger percentage of students with mothers (13.2%) working in technology than students with fathers (3.5%) working in technology. And, the majority of this sample did not report a disability.

The general demographic information from the whole sample was used as a foundation to compare CT students to NT students to then compare female and male students.

Research Question One:

What is the demographic profile of students who pursue computer technology careers and how does it compare with non-technology careers?

Demographics Profiles Comparing CT and NT Students

The sample profiles were divided into CT or NT groups. Each survey question was compared and analyzed in answer to research question number one.

Four hundred twenty-four students participated in this study. There were 173 (40.8%) students enrolled in CT programs and 251 (59.2%) students in NT programs. For this study, CT programs were defined as those in the following CareerTech career

clusters: Arts, AV Technology and Communications; Business, Management &

Administration; Information Technology; and Science, Technology, Engineering, and

Mathematics. Non-technology programs were those in the following CareerTech career

clusters: Agriculture, Food, & Natural Resources; Architecture & Construction;

Education & Training; Finance; Government & Public Administration; Health Science;

Hospitality & Tourism; Human Services; Law, Public Safety & Security; Manufacturing;

Marketing, Sales & Service; and Transportation, Distribution & Logistics.

The numbers of students and the percentages profiling the demographics of

students in CT and NT programs are shown in Table 9.

Table 9

Demographics for CT and NT Programs [a]

	Computer Technology			Non-Technology		
Gender:	CT Frequency (n=173)	CT Percentage (n=173)	Sample Percentage (N=424)	NT Frequency (n=251)	NT Percentage (n=251)	Sample Percentage (N=424)
Male	39	22.5%	9.2%	160	63.7%	37.7%
Female	134	77.5%	31.6%	91	36.3%	21.5%
Age:	CT Frequency	CT Percentage	Sample Percentage	NT Frequency	NT Percentage	Sample Percentage
18 and 19	61	35.3%	14.4%	186	74.1%	43.9%
20-29	37	21.4%	8.7%	37	14.7%	8.7%
30-39	31	17.9%	7.3%	13	5.2%	3.1%
40-49	32	18.5%	7.5%	8	3.2%	1.9%
50-59	10	5.8%	2.4%	7	2.8%	1.7%
60-88	2	1.2%	0.5%	0	0.0%	0.0%
Ethnicity:	CT Frequency	CT Percentage	Sample Percentage	NT Frequency	NT Percentage	Sample Percentage
Caucasian	111	64.2%	26.2%	177	70.5%	41.7%
African American	7	4.0%	1.7%	16	6.4%	3.8%
Native American	42	24.3%	9.9%	33	13.1%	7.8%
Asian	1	0.6%	0.2%	0	0.0%	0.0%
Hispanic	4	2.3%	0.9%	17	6.8%	4.0%
Latino	2	1.2%	0.5%	1	0.4%	0.2%
Multiracial	5	2.9%	1.2%	4	1.6%	0.9%
Other	1	0.6%	0.2%	3	1.2%	0.7%
Grade:	CT	CT	Sample	NT	NT	Sample

	Frequency	Percentage	Percentage	Frequency	Percentage	Percentage
HS Junior	20	11.6%	4.7%	84	33.5%	19.8%
HS Senior	22	12.7%	5.2%	78	31.1%	18.4%
Post-Sec	95	54.9%	22.4%	63	25.1%	14.9%
Other	36	20.8%	8.5%	26	10.4%	6.1%
Residence:	CT	CT	Sample	NT	NT	Sample
	Frequency	Percentage	Percentage	Frequency	Percentage	Percentage
Urban	0	0.0%	0.0%	15	6.0%	3.5%
Suburban	1	0.6%	0.2%	14	5.6%	3.3%
Town	114	65.9%	26.9%	127	50.6%	30.0%
Rural	58	33.5%	13.7%	95	37.8%	22.4%
Income:	CT	CT	Sample	NT	NT	Sample
	Frequency	Percentage	Percentage	Frequency	Percentage	Percentage
0-$9,999	91	52.6%	21.5%	90	35.9%	21.2%
$10,000-$19,999	30	17.3%	7.1%	15	6.0%	3.5%
$20,000 - $29,999	15	8.7%	3.5%	26	10.4%	6.1%
$30,000 - $39,999	11	6.4%	2.6%	31	12.4%	7.3%
$40,000 - $49,999	12	6.9%	2.8%	28	11.2%	6.6%
$50,000 - $59,999	6	3.5%	1.4%	17	6.8%	4.0%
$60,000 - $69,999	2	1.2%	0.5%	14	5.6%	3.3%
$70,000 - $79,999	2	1.2%	0.5%	12	4.8%	2.8%
$80,000 - $89,999	1	0.6%	0.2%	6	2.4%	1.4%
≥$90,000	3	1.7%	0.7%	12	4.8%	2.8%
Marital:	CT	CT	Sample	NT	NT	Sample
	Frequency	Percentage	Percentage	Frequency	Percentage	Percentage
Divorced	30	17.3%	7.1%	9	3.6%	2.1%
Married	45	26.0%	10.6%	20	8.0%	4.7%
Separated	10	5.8%	2.4%	4	1.6%	0.9%
Single	84	48.6%	19.8%	216	86.1%	50.9%
Widowed	4	2.3%	0.9%	2	0.8%	0.5%
Siblings:	CT	CT	Sample	NT	NT	Sample
	Frequency	Percentage	Percentage	Frequency	Percentage	Percentage
None	60	34.7%	14.2%	85	33.9%	20.0%
1	45	26.0%	10.6%	79	31.5%	18.6%
2	36	20.8%	8.5%	50	19.9%	11.8%
3	15	8.7%	3.5%	27	10.8%	6.4%
4 or more	17	9.8%	4.0%	10	4.0%	2.4%
Father in Technology:	CT	CT	Sample	NT	NT	Sample
	Frequency	Percentage	Percentage	Frequency	Percentage	Percentage
Yes	7	4.0%	1.7%	8	3.2%	1.9%
No	162	93.6%	38.2%	226	90.0%	53.3%
Not Sure	4	2.3%	0.9%	17	6.8%	4.0%
Mother in Technology:	CT	CT	Sample	NT	NT	Sample
	Frequency	Percentage	Percentage	Frequency	Percentage	Percentage
Yes	24	13.9%	5.7%	32	12.7%	7.5%
No	146	84.4%	34.4%	207	82.5%	48.8%
Not Sure	3	1.7%	0.7%	12	4.8%	2.8%

Counseling:	CT Frequency	CT Percentage	Sample Percentage	NT Frequency	NT Percentage	Sample Percentage
Dropout Recovery	0	0.0%	0.0%	2	0.8%	0.5%
TANF	24	13.9%	5.7%	13	5.2%	3.1%
Displaced Homemaker	5	2.9%	1.2%	1	0.4%	0.2%
None	131	75.7%	30.9%	224	89.2%	52.8%
Other	13	7.5%	3.1%	11	4.4%	2.6%
First Choice:	CT Frequency	CT Percentage	Sample Percentage	NT Frequency	NT Percentage	Sample Percentage
Yes	157	90.8%	37.0%	221	88.0%	52.1%
No	16	9.2%	3.8%	30	12.0%	7.1%
Selection Process:	CT Frequency	CT Percentage	Sample Percentage	NT Frequency	NT Percentage	Sample Percentage
Yes	32	18.5%	7.5%	34	13.5%	8.0%
No	141	81.5%	33.3%	217	86.5%	51.2%
Disabilities:[b]	CT Frequency	CT Percentage	Sample Percentage	NT Frequency	NT Percentage	Sample Percentage
Vision	16	9.2%	3.8%	17	6.8%	4.0%
Hearing	9	5.2%	2.1%	9	3.6%	2.1%
Motor Development	8	4.6%	1.9%	3	1.2%	0.7%
Cognitively Disadvantaged	4	2.3%	0.9%	2	0.8%	0.5%
Academically Disadvantaged	11	4.6%	2.6%	18	7.2%	4.2%
Economically Disadvantaged	25	14.5%	5.9%	13	5.2%	3.1%

[a]Rounding errors may have prevented percentages from equaling 100%.
[b]Students could select more than one disability.

Comparisons of Students in CT and NT Programs on Individual Demographic Variables

The sample for this study was almost equal between males and females with males represented by 53.1% and females represent by 46.9%. In answer to research question number one, students enrolled in CT programs were compared to NT students. Students enrolled in the CT programs were mostly female with 134 (77.5%) enrollees and only 39 (22.5%) males which were 9.2% of the total sample. By contrast, the NT students were 36.3% females and 63.7% males. Figure 1 shows gender comparisons for gender comparisons for CT and NT programs.

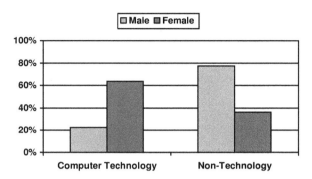

Figure 1. Comparing gender percentages of CT students to NT students.

The sample was 58.3% teenagers (18-19), but the division of CT and NT programs as shown in Figure 2 showed that 74.1% of the 18-19 years old students were in NT programs, which was 43.9% of the total sample. The percentage in CT was only 35.3%, which was 14.4% of the total sample. The CT programs had a larger percentage in their thirties, forties, fifties, and older than the NT programs. Computer technology had the two oldest students, who were 60 or 88.

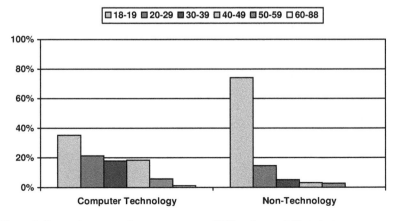

Figure 2. Comparing grouped age percentages of CT students to NT students.

The ethnic distribution of the sample showed the largest percentage being Caucasian, then Native American, African American, Hispanic, Multiracial, Other, Latino, and Asian being last with only one participant. The ethnic distribution by programs (See Figure 3) was consistent with the sample, as the largest percentage of both CT and NT programs were Caucasian. However, the NT percentage was almost 6% larger than the CT programs. The second largest percentage for both programs was Native Americans. Although Native Americans were the second largest ethnic group in the total sample and in both programs, the computer program contained a larger percentage than NT by over 10%. The only Asian student that participated in the study was enrolled in a CT program. NT students had more Hispanic students than African American, which was different from the sample and the CT programs. There were larger percentages of Caucasian, Hispanic, and Latino students in the NT programs than in the CT programs.

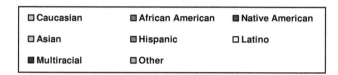

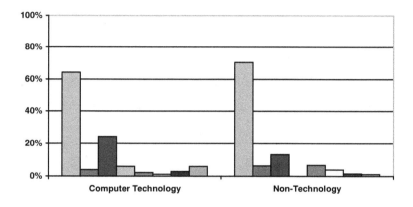

Figure 3. Comparing race percentages of CT students to NT students.

The sample grade level of students was almost equally divided between students still in high school and post-secondary students out of high school. However, as shown in Figure 4, among the students in CT programs 75.7% were post-secondary and only 24.3% were in high school, which was less than 10% of the total sample. By contrast, over 64% of the NT students were in high school as Juniors and Seniors, which was almost 40% of the total sample.

The students that reported "Other" were deemed to be post-secondary for both groups. The CT group was primarily out of high school and the NT group was primarily in high school.

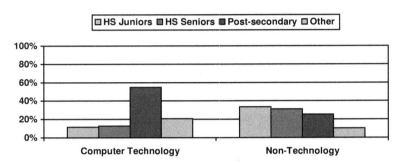

Figure 4. Comparing grade level percentages of CT students to NT students.

The student residency for the sample was largely from towns and rural areas (92.9%). Figure 5 shows that there was only one (0.6%) CT student from the metro areas while the NT had 29 (11.6%), but this was still consistent with the majority of students in that most of the participants were living in towns or rural areas in both CT and NT programs. A larger percentage of the participants lived in towns rather than rural areas in both CT and NT programs.

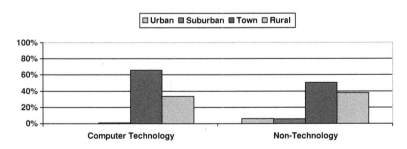

Figure 5. Comparing residence percentages of CT students to NT students.

As shown in Figure 6, there were more students in the lower income brackets in the CT programs and more from the higher income brackets in the NT programs. Almost

70% of the CT students had incomes under $20,000 while the NT students that had

incomes of over $20,000 were over 58%.

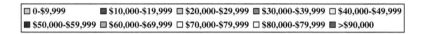

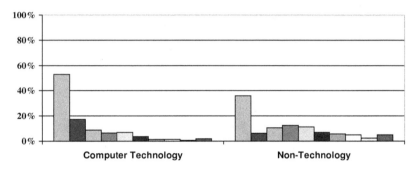

Figure 6. Comparing income percentages of CT students to NT students.

Figure 7 shows that both CT and NT students were mostly single, which matched

the pattern in the sample. However, 86.1% of the NT students were single which

represented 50.9% of the total sample. Although more CT students were single than

married, divorced, separated, or widowed, the single CT students were only 48.6%,

which was only 19.8% of the total sample. There were 26% that were married and over

17% that were divorced while the NT students consisted of 8% that were married and

3.6% that were divorced. There was a wider variety of marital status among CT than NT

students. There were few students that were widowed or separated in either CT or NT

programs.

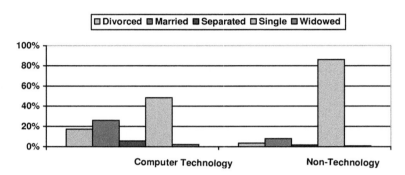

Figure 7. Comparing marital status percentages of CT students to NT students.

As shown in Figure 8, more of both the CT and the NT students did not have siblings at home than students that did have siblings at home. The one group that was different from the total sample was the CT group with 4 or more siblings at home. It was the only group that was larger than the NT students and represented 9.8% of the CT students to only 4% of the NT students.

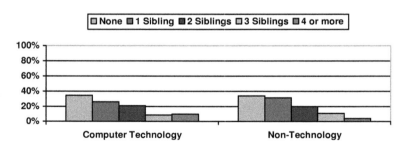

Figure 8. Comparing siblings at home percentages of CT students to NT students.

As shown in Figure 9, of the 15 (3.5%) that responded yes to whether their fathers worked in a technology field, seven (4%) were in the CT programs and eight (3.2%) were in the NT programs.

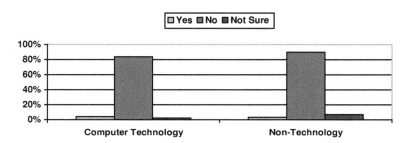

Figure 9. Comparing fathers in technology field percentages of CT students to NT students.

Figure 10 shows that of the 56 (13.2%) that responded yes to whether their mothers worked in a technology field, 24 (13.9%) were in the CT programs and 32 (12.7%) were in the NT programs.

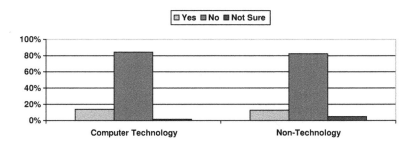

Figure 10. Comparing mothers in technology field percentages of CT students to NT students.

Figure 11 summarizes the percentage of CT and NT students who reported parents working in a technology field. This shows that parental employment in technology was not large for either of the groups. However, for students in both CT and NT programs who did have a parent in technology, this was more frequently a mother rather than a father.

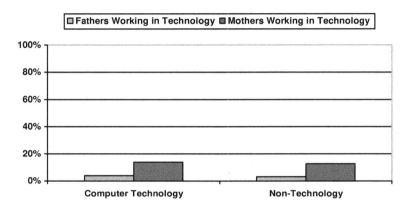

Figure 11. Comparing fathers and mothers working in a technology field percentages of male and female CT students.

Of the 37 (8.8%) from the total sample that responded that they had received career guidance through TANF, 24 (5.7%) were in the CT programs and 13 (3.1%) were in the NT programs (See Figure 12). The two that were in a Dropout Recovery Program were both in the NT programs. Of the six (1.4%) listed as Displaced Homemakers, five (1.2%) were in the CT programs and 1 (0.4%) was in a NT program. The majority of students in both of the programs did not participate in career guidance programs, but over 10% more of the CT students did participate in career guidance than NT. The largest percentage of the CT students participating in some form of assistance and career guidance, had participated in the TANF program.

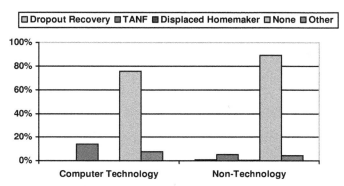

Figure 12. Comparing career counseling percentages of CT students to NT students.

The CT students that reported a different type of counseling or career guidance listed vocational rehabilitation, Education Enhancement Center, ASCOG, and Social Security. The NT students that listed "Other" expanded in the comment section identifying vocational rehabilitation, Education Enhancement Center, anger management, military, and workforce as other sources of counseling. Both groups were primarily attending the programs without counseling assistance or guidance from available sources.

As shown in Figure 13, most students in both CT programs and NT programs were admitted into their first choice program. Almost 3% more NT than CT students were not admitted to their first choice of programs offered at the CareerTech. Students that selected "No" on the survey had an opportunity to comment. Three of the CT students commented that they wanted LPN but did not elaborate on why they did not get in the program. One indicated that they want medical billing and coding. Another wanted medical technician, while one reported that they were too late for their first choice without commenting on what their first choice was. The NT group had more that listed comments. Two listed "Second" that may have indicated that their current program was a second choice but did not list what program was their first choice. Other programs that were listed were wood shop, radio broadcasting, aviation maintenance and engineering, welding, heat and air, auto tech, health science, auto paint and body, machine tool, and diesel mechanic. One comment was "I wanted to learn about cars" and another comment was "medical administration, but I didn't like it." Both groups generally were admitted into a program of their choice, and this pattern was nearly identical for the CT and NT groups.

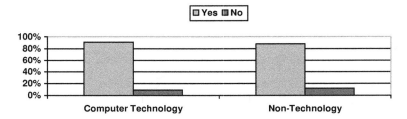

Figure 13. Comparing first choice percentages of CT students to NT students.

A slightly larger percentage of the CT students had a selection process to be admitted into a program than the NT students (See Figure 14). Of the 173 CT students, 18.5% went through some sort of selection process while 13.5% of the 251 NT students went through a selection process.

There was a comment section on the survey for students to explain or comment on the selection process. Two students reported that they had to interview for the computer repair program. One student listed TABE SAGE as the process for their program which was "Computers."

Two of the NT students that listed welding as their program involvement, listed placement test in the comment section. One NT student reported that there was an interview for acceptance in the health careers – massage therapy. Both groups primarily were not required to go through a process for acceptance. This pattern was very similar for CT and NT programs, although slightly more CT students did have a selection process.

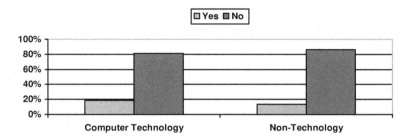

Figure 14. Comparing selection process percentages of CT students to NT students.

Figure 15 shows the disabilities reported by CT and NT students. There were 73 (42.2%) CT students and 62 (24.7%) NT students that reported a disability or disadvantage. There was a higher percentage in five of the six areas of disabilities in the CT programs than the NT programs: vision; hearing; motor development; cognitively disadvantaged; and economically disadvantaged. Academically disadvantaged was the only one that reported a higher percentage of NT students than CT students.

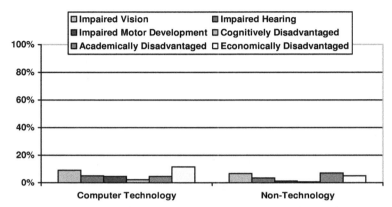

Figure 15. Comparing disabilities and disadvantages percentages of CT students to NT students.

The percentage of students with visual and hearing disabilities were almost equal in number for both groups. There was a sizable discrepancy between CT and NT students with economically disadvantages. The groups generally reported no disability or disadvantage, but CT students had a higher percentage and greater variety of reported disadvantages overall than NT students.

Summary of Demographics Profiles Comparing CT and NT Students

The CT and NT groups were very similar to each other and to the whole sample in many ways and several demographic variables did not discriminate between the groups. However, the demographic profiles for the CT and NT students were somewhat different for gender, age, marital status, grade level, and income. The CT students were mostly female, post-secondary, with family incomes of less than $20,000 per year. The CT students were to some extent older than NT students and showed greater variability in age range and marital status. There were larger percentages that were married, divorced, separated, or widowed in the CT than in the NT programs. This may have been related to the larger range of ages that characterized this group. The NT students were mostly male, young, single, high school students, with family incomes of more than $20,000 per year.

Both groups were mostly Caucasians, residing in small towns or rural areas, and admitted in the program of choice without a selection process. However, the pattern of ethnic minorities was different for the two groups. The Asian and American Indian students were predominantly in the CT while African Americans, Hispanic, and Latino students were more concentrated in the NT programs. Most of both groups did not have siblings at home or parents that worked in a technology field.

Research Question Two:

Are those demographic profiles the same for males and females?

Both the CT and NT groups were next separated by gender to determine if the demographic profiles were the same for female and male students in either or both groups. The division by gender was used to answer research question number two. The demographical data for both the CT and NT programs were divided by gender and presented in Tables 10-13. The data related to females in a CT program are shown in Table 10, and the data for males in a CT program are shown in Table 11.

Demographics Profiles Comparing Male and Female CT Students

There were 173 CT students enrolled in four (Arts, A/V Technology and Communications; Business, Management & Administration; Information Technology; and Science, Technology, Engineering, and Mathematics) of the 16 career clusters. Those 173 student profiles were compared and analyzed by gender to answer research question number two for the CT group.

Of the 173 students enrolled in a CT program, 134 were female. The sample

percentage, CT percentage, gender percentage, and frequency of the female technology

students are shown in Table 10.

Table 10

Demographics Profile for Females Attending CT Programs

Females Attending CT Programs				
	Female Frequency (n=134)	Female Percentage (n=134)	CT Percentage (n=173)	Sample Percentage[a] (N=424)
Age:				
18-19	38	28.4%	22.0%	9.0%
20-29	32	23.9%	18.5%	7.5%
30-39	29	21.6%	16.8%	6.8%
40-49	24	17.9%	13.9%	5.7%
50-59	10	7.5%	5.8%	2.4%
60-88	1	0.7%	0.6%	0.2%
Ethnicity:	Female Frequency	Female Percentage	CT Percentage	Sample Percentage
Caucasian	89	66.4%	51.4%	21.0%
African American	3	2.2%	1.7%	0.7%
Native American	33	24.6%	19.1%	7.8%
Asian	1	0.7%	0.6%	0.2%
Hispanic	3	2.2%	1.7%	0.7%
Latino	1	0.7%	0.6%	0.2%
Multiracial	3	2.2%	1.7%	0.7%
Other	1	0.7%	0.6%	0.2%
Grade:	Female Frequency	Female Percentage	CT Percentage	Sample Percentage
HS Junior	10	7.5%	5.8%	2.4%
HS Senior	12	9.0%	6.9%	2.8%
Post-Secondary	83	61.9%	48.0%	19.6%
Other	29	21.6%	16.8%	6.8%
Residence Area:	Female Frequency	Female Percentage	CT Percentage	Sample Percentage
Urban	0	0.0%	0.0%	0.0%
Suburban	1	0.7%	0.6%	0.2%
Town	81	60.4%	46.8%	19.1%
Rural	52	38.8%	30.1%	12.3%
Income:	Female Frequency	Female Percentage	CT Percentage	Sample Percentage
0-$9,999	74	55.2%	42.8%	17.5%

		Frequency	Female Percentage	CT Percentage	Sample Percentage
	$10,000-$19,999	23	17.2%	13.3%	5.4%
	$20,000-$29,999	14	10.4%	8.1%	3.3%
	$30,000-$39,999	6	4.5%	3.5%	1.4%
	$40,000-$49,999	6	4.5%	3.5%	1.4%
	$50,000-$59,999	4	3.0%	2.3%	0.9%
	$60,000-$69,999	2	1.5%	1.2%	0.5%
	$70,000-$79,999	2	1.5%	1.2%	0.5%
	$80,000-$89,999	1	0.7%	0.6%	0.2%
	≥$90,000	2	1.5%	1.2%	0.5%
Marital:		Female Frequency	Female Percentage	CT Percentage	Sample Percentage
	Divorced	25	18.7%	14.5%	5.9%
	Married	41	30.6%	23.7%	9.7%
	Separated	10	7.5%	5.8%	2.4%
	Single	55	41.0%	31.8%	13.0%
	Widowed	3	2.2%	1.7%	0.7%
Siblings at home:		Female Frequency	Female Percentage	CT Percentage	Sample Percentage
	None	41	30.6%	23.7%	9.7%
	1	35	26.1%	20.2%	8.3%
	2	32	23.9%	18.5%	7.5%
	3	12	9.0%	6.9%	2.8%
	4 or more	14	10.4%	8.1%	3.3%
Father in a technology field:		Female Frequency	Female Percentage	CT Percentage	Sample Percentage
	Yes	4	3.0%	2.3%	0.9%
	No	126	94.0%	72.8%	29.7%
	Not Sure	4	3.0%	2.3%	0.9%
Mother in technology field:		Female Frequency	Female Percentage	CT Percentage	Sample Percentage
	Yes	16	11.9%	9.2%	3.8%
	No	118	88.1%	68.2%	27.8%
	Not Sure	0	0.0%	0.0%	0.0%
Counseling:		Female Frequency	Female Percentage	CT Percentage	Sample Percentage
	Dropout Recovery	0	0.0%	0.0%	0.0%
	TANF	23	17.2%	13.3%	5.4%
	Displaced Homemaker	4	3.0%	2.3%	0.9%
	None	95	70.9%	54.9%	22.4%
	Other	12	9.0%	6.9%	2.8%
First choice:		Female Frequency	Female Percentage	CT Percentage	Sample Percentage
	Yes	119	88.8%	68.8%	28.1%
	No	15	11.2%	8.7%	3.5%
Selection Process:		Female Frequency	Female Percentage	CT Percentage	Sample Percentage

Yes	27	20.1%	15.6%	6.4%
No	107	79.9%	61.8%	25.2%
Disabilities:[b]	Female Frequency	Female Percentage	CT Percentage	Sample Percentage
Vision	10	7.5%	5.8%	2.4%
Hearing	6	4.5%	3.5%	1.4%
Motor Development	4	3.0%	2.3%	0.9%
Cognitively Disadvantaged	2	1.5%	1.2%	0.5%
Academically Disadvantaged	8	6.0%	4.6%	1.9%
Economically Disadvantaged	20	14.9%	11.6%	4.7%

[a]Rounding errors may have prevented percentage from equaling 100%.
[b]Students could select more than one disability.

There were 39 males enrolled in a CT program. Sample percentages, CT

programs percentages, and gender percentages and frequencies are shown in Table 11 for

males in the CT programs.

Table 11

Demographics Profiles for Males Attending CT Programs

	Males in CT Programs			
	Male Frequency (n=39)	Male Percentage (n=39)	CT Percentage (n=173)	Sample Percentage[a] (N=424)
Age:				
18-19	23	59.0%	13.3%	5.4%
20-29	5	12.8%	2.9%	1.2%
30-39	2	5.1%	1.2%	0.5%
40-49	8	20.5%	4.6%	1.9%
50-59	0	0.0%	0.0%	0.0%
60-88	1	2.6%	0.6%	0.2%
Ethnicity:	Male Frequency	Male Percentage	CT Percentage	Sample Percentage
Caucasian	22	56.4%	12.7%	5.2%
African American	4	10.3%	2.3%	0.9%
Native American	9	23.1%	5.2%	2.1%
Asian	0	0.0%	0.0%	0.0%
Hispanic	1	2.6%	0.6%	0.2%
Latino	1	2.6%	0.6%	0.2%
Multiracial	2	5.1%	1.2%	0.5%
Other	0	0.0%	0.0%	0.0%
Grade:	Male Frequency	Male Percentage	CT Percentage	Sample Percentage

		Male Frequency	Male Percentage	CT Percentage	Sample Percentage
	HS Junior	10	25.6%	5.8%	2.4%
	HS Senior	10	25.6%	5.8%	2.4%
	Post-Secondary	12	30.8%	6.9%	2.8%
	Other	7	17.9%	4.0%	1.7%
Residence Area:		Male Frequency	Male Percentage	CT Percentage	Sample Percentage
	Urban	0	0.0%	0.0%	0.0%
	Suburban	0	0.0%	0.0%	0.0%
	Town	33	84.6%	19.1%	7.8%
	Rural	6	15.4%	3.5%	1.4%
Income:		Male Frequency	Male Percentage	CT Percentage	Sample Percentage
	0-$9,999	17	43.6%	9.8%	4.0%
	$10,000-$19,999	7	17.9%	4.0%	1.7%
	$20,000-$29,999	1	2.6%	0.6%	0.2%
	$30,000-$39,999	5	12.8%	2.9%	1.2%
	$40,000-$49,999	6	15.4%	3.5%	1.4%
	$50,000-$59,999	2	5.1%	1.2%	0.5%
	$60,000-$69,999	0	0.0%	0.0%	0.0%
	$70,000-$79,999	0	0.0%	0.0%	0.0%
	$80,000-$89,999	0	0.0%	0.0%	0.0%
	≥$90,000	1	2.6%	0.6%	0.2%
Marital:		Male Frequency	Male Percentage	CT Percentage	Sample Percentage
	Divorced	5	12.8%	2.9%	1.2%
	Married	4	10.3%	2.3%	0.9%
	Separated	0	0.0%	0.0%	0.0%
	Single	29	74.4%	16.8%	6.8%
	Widowed	1	2.6%	0.6%	0.2%
Siblings at home:		Male Frequency	Male Percentage	CT Percentage	Sample Percentage
	None	19	48.7%	11.0%	4.5%
	1	10	25.6%	5.8%	2.4%
	2	4	10.3%	2.3%	0.9%
	3	3	7.7%	1.7%	0.7%
	4 or more	3	7.7%	1.7%	0.7%
Father in a technology field:		Male Frequency	Male Percentage	CT Percentage	Sample Percentage
	Yes	3	7.7%	1.7%	0.7%
	No	36	92.3%	20.8%	8.5%
	Not Sure	0	0.0%	0.0%	0.0%
Mother in technology field:		Male Frequency	Male Percentage	CT Percentage	Sample Percentage
	Yes	8	20.5%	4.6%	1.9%
	No	28	71.8%	16.2%	6.6%
	Not Sure	3	7.7%	1.7%	0.7%

Counseling:	Male Frequency	Male Percentage	CT Percentage	Sample Percentage
Dropout Recovery	0	0.0%	0.0%	0.0%
TANF	1	2.6%	0.6%	0.2%
Displaced Homemaker	1	2.6%	0.6%	0.2%
None	36	92.3%	20.8%	8.5%
Other	1	2.6%	0.6%	0.2%
First choice:	Male Frequency	Male Percentage	CT Percentage	Sample Percentage
Yes	38	97.4%	22.0%	9.0%
No	1	2.6%	0.6%	0.2%
Selection Process:	Male Frequency	Male Percentage	CT Percentage	Sample Percentage
Yes	5	12.8%	2.9%	1.2%
No	34	87.2%	19.7%	8.0%
Disabilities: [b]	Male Frequency	Male Percentage	CT Percentage	Sample Percentage
Impaired Vision	6	15.4%	3.5%	1.4%
Impaired Hearing	3	7.7%	1.7%	0.7%
Impaired Motor Development	4	10.3%	2.3%	0.9%
Cognitively Disadvantaged	2	5.1%	1.2%	0.5%
Academically Disadvantaged	3	7.7%	1.7%	0.7%
Economically Disadvantaged	5	12.8%	2.9%	1.2%

[a]Rounding errors may have prevented percentage from equaling 100%.
[b]Students could select more than one disability.

Gender Comparisons in CT Programs on Individual Demographic Variables

Data from Tables 10 and 11 about males and females in CT programs were

compared for gender variance and similarity. As shown in Figure 16, the ages of students

in the CT programs, as in the sample as a whole, were largely 18-19 years for both males

and females; however, the percent of male students (59%) that were 18-19 years old was

much higher than the percentage for the females (28.4%). As the ages of the CT students

increased, the percentage of students was smaller in each group except for males in their

forties. That group of CT males in their forties was 20.5% and was second only to the 18-

19 year old students. That group was larger than the groups of twenties and thirties,

which was different from the sample and the CT group as a whole. There were no males in the fifties group and only one male over sixty. These data show that females were more evenly spread across age groups and showed greater age range.

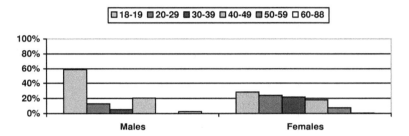

Figure 16. Comparing grouped age percentages of male and female CT students.

Ethic composition of males and females are compared in Figure 17. The majority of both females and males in the CT programs were Caucasian as was true for the sample and both the CT programs and the NT programs. However, there were a larger percentage of females than males that were Caucasian. The percentage of male African Americans and multiracial students was higher than the percentage for females. The percentage was about the same for male and female Native American and Hispanic students. There was only one Asian student and she was a female in a CT program. While males and females were generally Caucasian in CT programs, this trend was more pronounced for females than for males.

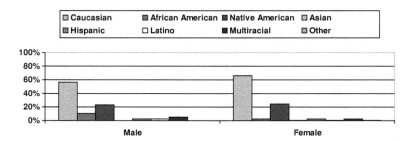

Figure 17. Comparing race percentages of male and female CT students.

As shown in Figure 18, females in high school were less than males in high school and more than males in post-secondary levels. The percentage of male students in CT programs that were in high school was 51.2% and females were only 16.5%. Thus the female CT students tended to be older than the males.

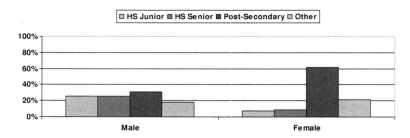

Figure 18. Comparing grade level percentages of male and female CT students.

Figure 19 compares males and females in CT programs based on their residence. The CT programs had only one (0.6%) student from the metro areas. However, since the sample had so few representatives from Metro areas, this is not conclusive. Only 15% of the male students were from rural areas while 38.8% of the female students were from rural areas. The sample had 36.1% from the rural areas. Almost 85% of the male students were from a town compared to only 60% of the females, while the sample had 56.8%

from towns.

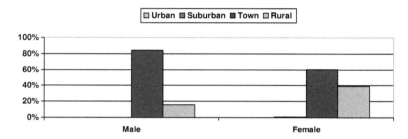

Figure 19. Comparing residence percentages of male and female CT students.

Comparative family incomes for males and females in CT programs are shown in

Figure 20. Over half of the females in the CT programs had family incomes of less than

$10,000, which represented 42.8% of the CT students, and 17.5% of the sample. By

contrast, only 5.2% of the females had family incomes of more than $60,000 and only

2.6% of the males had family incomes of over $60,000. Only 9% of the females in the CT

programs were in the $30,000-$50,000 range compared to 28.2% of the males had family

incomes in the $3,000 to $50,000 range. These data showed that the CT students of both

genders tended to have relatively low family incomes, but this was especially true for the

females.

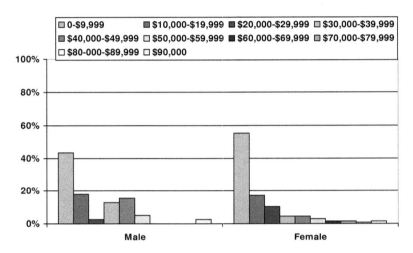

Figure 20. Comparing income percentages of male and female CT students.

As shown in Figure 21, both female and male students in the CT programs reported a larger percentage of single students than married, separated, divorced, or widowed. The males were 74.4% single and females were 41% single. Married females represented over 30% and divorced females represented 18.7%. There were more divorced males (12.8%) than married males (10.3%).

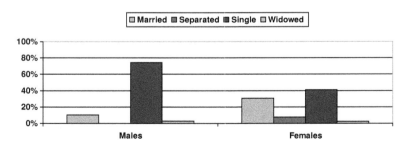

Figure 21. Comparing marital status percentages of male and female CT students.

Figure 22 reveals that almost half of the male students did not have a sibling at home, whereas less than a third of the female students did not have a sibling at home. A larger percentage of the female students had siblings at home than the male students, with the largest percentage for both groups being one sibling and increasingly fewer as the number of siblings increased.

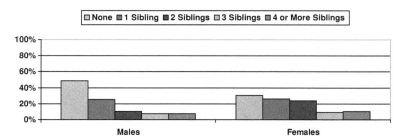

Figure 22. Comparing siblings at home percentages of male and female CT students.

Figures 23 and 24 compare parental employment in a technology field for male and female technology students. As shown in Figure 23, a larger percentage of the males had fathers working in technology than females, but the percentage of fathers working in technology fields was still negligible. No male students were unsure of their father's career employment and only 3.0% of the female students were unsure if their fathers worked in technology. Neither groups reported very many fathers that worked in a technology field.

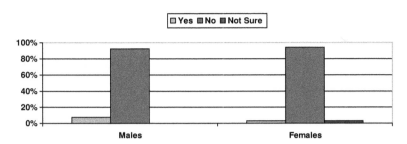

Figure 23. Comparing fathers in technology field percentages of male and female CT students.

Table 24 shows that there was a higher percentage of CT males than females with mothers working in a technology field, but the percentage was again low. No females listed that they were unsure of whether their mothers worked in technology or not and only 1.9% of the males were unsure. Generally most of the mothers of both females and males did not work in technology.

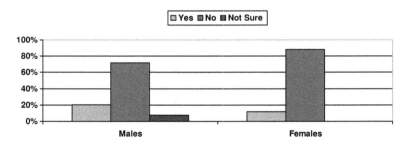

Figure 24. Comparing mothers in technology field percentages of male and female CT students.

Parental employment in technology is summarized in Figure 25. This shows that while most CT students of both genders did not have a parent working in a technology field, the percentage of mothers working in technology fields was larger than fathers working in technology for both genders. There were more males with parents working in technology than females.

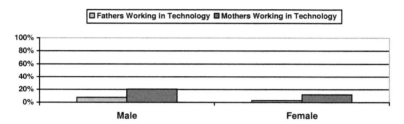

Figure 25. Comparing fathers and mothers working in a technology field percentages of male and female CT students.

As shown in Figure 26, over 20% more females received some form of career counseling than the males. The largest percent of females that did receive counseling listed TANF as the form of assistance. There were only three CT males that received guidance assistance, with none participating in the Dropout Recovery Program. Of the five CT students that selected Displaced Homemakers as a form of career counseling, four (3%) were female and 1 (2.6%) was male. There were more females that selected "Other." The only male that made a comment typed in "All help I can Get." The females listed displaced worker, vocational rehabilitation, social security, and Education Enhancement Center. Most of both males and females reported no assistance or career counseling through specified programs.

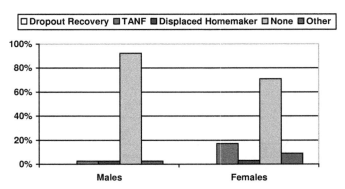

Figure 26. Comparing career counseling percentages of male and female CT students.

As shown in Figure 27, most males and females were admitted into their first

choice of programs. In fact, there was only one male (2.6%) not admitted into his first

choice, but he made no comment as to what was his first choice or why he was not

admitted into that program. He was the 88 year old displaced homemaker and is currently

in the information technology program. There were 15 (11.2%) females not admitted into

their first choice of programs. Several of the 15 listed that their first choice was the LNP

program but were in a different program. One reported that she was in information

technology but was changing to web design. One wrote that she was going to do

cosmetology but did computers instead. Both genders generally reported being admitted

to their first choice of programs.

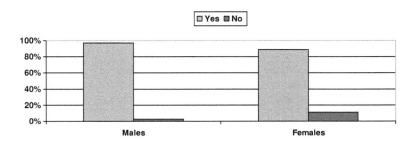

Figure 27. Comparing first choice percentages of male and female CT students.

Figure 28 shows that most of both males and females did not have a selection process to be admitted into a CT programs. Of the ones that did go through a selection process, the females had a higher percentage than the males. The majority of both gender groups did not experience a selection process.

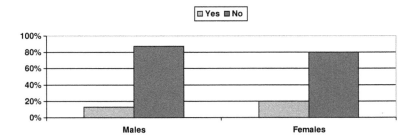

Figure 28. Comparing selection process percentages of male and female CT students.

Figure 29 reports the disabilities reported by males and females in CT programs. There were 50 (37.3%) of the 134 CT female students and 23 (59.0%) of the 39 CT male students that reported a form of disability or a disadvantage. Males listed vision as the most common area of disabilities. Males had a higher percentage than females in all areas except economically disadvantaged. Economically disadvantaged percentage was higher for females than for males, but only by a small percentage. Generally neither males nor

females in CT programs reported a disability or disadvantage.

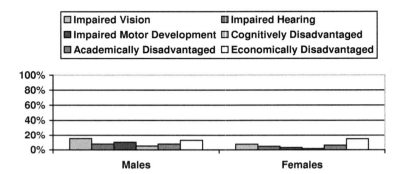

Figure 29. Comparing disabilities percentages of male and female CT students.

Summary of Demographics Profiles Comparing Male and Female CT Students

Computer technology students were generally young, especially the males.

Females were more evenly spread across age groups and had greater age range. A large

percent of both males and females were Caucasian. Native Americans were the next

largest group and were almost equal for males and females.

The males were almost evenly divided in the four grade levels: High School

Juniors; High School Seniors; Post-Secondary; and Other. The females were mostly Post-

Secondary students. Both males and females were primarily from towns and in a low

social-economic bracket. Males had a greater frequency of higher income brackets. Both

genders were predominantly single with few or no siblings at home. Very few had

parents working in technology, but there were more males than females with parents

working in technology. Most CT students of both genders did not receive career

counseling, but were able to enroll in their first choice of programs. There was not a selection process for most CT students and most did not have a disability or

disadvantage.

Demographics Profiles Comparing Male and Female NT Students

        There were 251 NT student responses that were compared and analyzed to answer

research question number two for the NT group. Demographic statistics for female NT

students are shown in Table 12 and compared to statistics for males as shown in Table

13.

Table 12

Demographics Profiles for Females Attending NT Programs

	Females in NT Programs			
	Female Frequency (n=91)	Female Percentage (n=91)	NT Percentage (n=251)	Sample Percentage[a] (N=424)
Age:				
18-19	53	58.2%	21.1%	12.5%
20-29	16	17.6%	6.4%	3.8%
30-39	9	9.9%	3.6%	2.1%
40-49	7	7.7%	2.8%	1.7%
50-59	6	6.6%	2.4%	1.4%
60-88	0	0.0%	0.0%	0.0%
Ethnicity:	Female Frequency	Female Percentage	NT Percentage	Sample Percentage
Caucasian	60	65.9%	23.9%	14.2%
African American	11	12.1%	4.4%	2.6%
Native American	14	15.4%	5.6%	3.3%
Asian	0	0.0%	0.0%	0.0%
Hispanic	3	3.3%	1.2%	0.7%
Latino	0	0.0%	0.0%	0.0%
Multiracial	2	2.2%	0.8%	0.5%
Other	1	1.1%	0.4%	0.2%
Grade:	Female Frequency	Female Percentage	NT Percentage	Sample Percentage
HS Junior	26	28.6%	10.4%	6.1%
HS Senior	20	22.0%	8.0%	4.7%
Post-Secondary	33	36.3%	13.1%	7.8%
Other	12	13.2%	4.8%	2.8%
Residence Area:	Female Frequency	Female Percentage	NT Percentage	Sample Percentage
Urban	10	11.0%	4.0%	2.4%
Suburban	9	9.9%	3.6%	2.1%
Town	47	51.6%	18.7%	11.1%
Rural	25	27.5%	10.0%	5.9%
Income:	Female	Female	NT Percentage	Sample

	Frequency	Percentage		Percentage
0-$9,999	44	48.4%	17.5%	10.4%
$10,000-$19,999	7	7.7%	2.8%	1.7%
$20,000-$29,999	9	9.9%	3.6%	2.1%
$30,000-$39,999	12	13.2%	4.8%	2.8%
$40,000-$49,999	10	11.0%	4.0%	2.4%
$50,000-$59,999	1	1.1%	0.4%	0.2%
$60,000-$69,999	2	2.2%	0.8%	0.5%
$70,000-$79,999	4	4.4%	1.6%	0.9%
$80,000-$89,999	1	1.1%	0.4%	0.2%
≥$90,000	1	1.1%	0.4%	0.2%
Marital:	Female Frequency	Female Percentage	NT Percentage	Sample Percentage
Divorced	7	7.7%	2.8%	1.7%
Married	13	14.3%	5.2%	3.1%
Separated	2	2.2%	0.8%	0.5%
Single	67	73.6%	26.7%	15.8%
Widowed	2	2.2%	0.8%	0.5%
Siblings at home:	Female Frequency	Female Percentage	NT Percentage	Sample Percentage
None	33	36.3%	13.1%	7.8%
1	22	24.2%	8.8%	5.2%
2	17	18.7%	6.8%	4.0%
3	15	16.5%	6.0%	3.5%
4 or more	4	4.4%	1.6%	0.9%
Father in a technology field:	Female Frequency	Female Percentage	NT Percentage	Sample Percentage
Yes	4	4.4%	1.6%	0.9%
No	79	86.8%	31.5%	18.6%
Not Sure	8	8.8%	3.2%	1.9%
Mother in technology field:	Female Frequency	Female Percentage	NT Percentage	Sample Percentage
Yes	9	9.9%	3.6%	2.1%
No	79	86.8%	31.5%	18.6%
Not Sure	3	3.3%	1.2%	0.7%
Counseling:	Female Frequency	Female Percentage	NT Percentage	Sample Percentage
Dropout Recovery	0	0.0%	0.0%	0.0%
TANF	11	12.1%	4.4%	2.6%
Displaced Homemaker	1	1.1%	0.4%	0.2%
None	75	82.4%	29.9%	17.7%
Other	4	4.4%	1.6%	0.9%
First choice:	Female Frequency	Female Percentage	NT Percentage	Sample Percentage
Yes	79	86.8%	31.5%	18.6%
No	12	13.2%	4.8%	2.8%
Selection Process:	Female Frequency	Female Percentage	NT Percentage	Sample Percentage
Yes	19	20.9%	7.6%	4.5%
No	72	79.1%	28.7%	17.0%
Disabilities: [b]	Female Frequency	Female Percentage	NT Percentage	Sample Percentage
Impaired Vision	6	6.6%	2.4%	1.4%
Impaired Hearing	5	5.5%	2.0%	1.2%
Impaired Motor Development	1	1.1%	0.4%	0.2%

108

Cognitively Disadvantaged	1	1.1%	0.4%	0.2%
Academically Disadvantaged	12	15.2%	4.8%	2.8%
Economically Disadvantaged	1	1.1%	0.4%	0.2%

[a]Rounding errors may have prevented percentages from equaling 100%.
[b]Students could select more than one disability.

Table 13

Demographics Profiles for Males Attending NT Programs

	Males in NT Programs			
	Male Frequency (n=160)	Male Percentage (n=160)	NT Percentage (n=251)	Sample Percentage[a] (N=424)
Age:				
18-19	133	83.1%	53.0%	31.4%
20-29	21	13.1%	8.4%	5.0%
30-39	4	2.5%	1.6%	0.9%
40-49	1	0.6%	0.4%	0.2%
50-59	1	0.6%	0.4%	0.2%
60-88	0	0.0%	0.0%	0.0%
Ethnicity:	Male Frequency	Male Percentage	NT Percentage	Sample Percentage
Caucasian	117	73.1%	46.6%	27.6%
African American	5	3.1%	2.0%	1.2%
Native American	19	11.9%	7.6%	4.5%
Asian	0	0.0%	0.0%	0.0%
Hispanic	14	8.8%	5.6%	3.3%
Latino	1	0.6%	0.4%	0.2%
Multiracial	2	1.3%	0.8%	0.5%
Other	2	1.3%	0.8%	0.5%
Grade:	Male Frequency	Male Percentage	NT Percentage	Sample Percentage
HS Junior	58	36.3%	23.1%	13.7%
HS Senior	58	36.3%	23.1%	13.7%
Post-Secondary	30	18.8%	12.0%	7.1%
Other	14	8.8%	5.6%	3.3%
Residence Area:	Male Frequency	Male Percentage	NT Percentage	Sample Percentage
Urban	5	3.1%	2.0%	1.2%
Suburban	5	3.1%	2.0%	1.2%
Town	80	50.0%	31.9%	18.9%
Rural	70	43.8%	27.9%	16.5%
Income:	Male Frequency	Male Percentage	NT Percentage	Sample Percentage
0-$9,999	46	28.8%	18.3%	10.9%
$10,000-$19,999	8	5.0%	3.2%	1.9%
$20,000-$29,999	17	10.6%	6.8%	4.0%
$30,000-$39,999	19	11.9%	7.6%	4.5%
$40,000-$49,999	18	11.3%	7.2%	4.3%
$50,000-$59,999	16	10.0%	6.4%	3.8%
$60,000-$69,999	12	7.5%	4.8%	2.8%
$70,000-$79,999	8	5.0%	3.2%	1.9%
$80,000-$89,999	5	3.1%	2.0%	1.2%

		Male Frequency	Male Percentage	NT Percentage	Sample Percentage
	≥$90,000	11	6.9%	4.4%	2.6%
Marital:		Male Frequency	Male Percentage	NT Percentage	Sample Percentage
	Divorced	2	1.3%	0.8%	0.5%
	Married	7	4.4%	2.8%	1.7%
	Separated	2	1.3%	0.8%	0.5%
	Single	149	93.1%	59.4%	35.1%
	Widowed	0	0.0%	0.0%	0.0%
Siblings at home:		Male Frequency	Male Percentage	NT Percentage	Sample Percentage
	None	52	32.5%	20.7%	12.3%
	1	57	35.6%	22.7%	13.4%
	2	33	20.6%	13.1%	7.8%
	3	12	7.5%	4.8%	2.8%
	4 or more	6	3.8%	2.4%	1.4%
Father in a technology field:		Male Frequency	Male Percentage	NT Percentage	Sample Percentage
	Yes	4	2.5%	1.6%	0.9%
	No	147	91.9%	58.6%	34.7%
	Not Sure	9	5.6%	3.6%	2.1%
Mother in technology field:		Male Frequency	Male Percentage	NT Percentage	Sample Percentage
	Yes	23	14.4%	9.2%	5.4%
	No	128	80.0%	51.0%	30.2%
	Not Sure	9	5.6%	3.6%	2.1%
Counseling:		Male Frequency	Male Percentage	NT Percentage	Sample Percentage
	Dropout Recovery	2	1.3%	0.8%	0.5%
	TANF	2	1.3%	0.8%	0.5%
	Displaced Homemaker	0	0.0%	0.0%	0.0%
	None	149	93.1%	59.4%	35.1%
	Other	7	4.4%	2.8%	1.7%
First choice:		Male Frequency	Male Percentage	NT Percentage	Sample Percentage
	Yes	142	88.8%	56.6%	33.5%
	No	18	11.3%	7.2%	4.2%
Selection Process:		Male Frequency	Male Percentage	NT Percentage	Sample Percentage
	Yes	15	9.4%	6.0%	3.5%
	No	145	90.6%	57.8%	34.2%
Disabilities: [b]		Male Frequency	Male Percentage	NT Percentage	Sample Percentage
	Impaired Vision	11	6.9%	4.4%	2.6%
	Impaired Hearing	4	2.5%	1.6%	0.9%
	Impaired Motor Development	2	1.3%	0.8%	0.5%
	Cognitively Disadvantaged	1	0.6%	0.4%	0.2%
	Academically Disadvantaged	6	3.8%	2.4%	1.4%
	Economically Disadvantaged	12	7.5%	4.8%	2.8%

[a]Rounding errors may have prevented percentage from equaling 100%.
[b]Students could select more than one disability.

Gender Comparisons in NT Programs on Individual Demographic Variables

Data from female students in NT programs, listed in Table 12, and data from male students in NT programs, listed in Table 13, were compared for variance and similarity. As shown in Figure 30, the ages of students in the NT programs were largely 18-19 years old, for both males and females. The percent of male students that were 18-19 year old was over 20% higher than the percentage for the females. There were only six (3.7%) male students in the 30 and over age brackets, with over 96% below 30 years of age. There were no males above their thirties. Females were more evenly spread across age groups and showed greater age range.

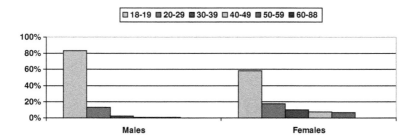

Figure 30. Comparing grouped age percentages of male and female NT students.

In comparing the ethnicity (See Figure 31) of the genders, the majority of females and males in the NT programs were Caucasian. There was a larger percentage of males than females that were Caucasian. There were more Hispanic males than females. The percentage of female African Americans students was higher than the percentage for males. There were no Asian or Latino females in a NT program. There were no Asian male students.

111

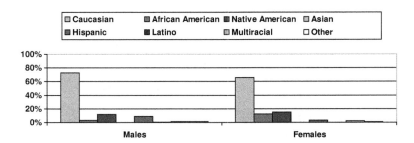

Figure 31. Comparing race percentage of male and female NT students.

As shown in Figure 32, the percentage of NT male students in high school was over 20% higher than female students. Female students were almost fifty percent high school students and fifty percent post-secondary students. Females in high school were less than males in high school and more than males in post-secondary levels.

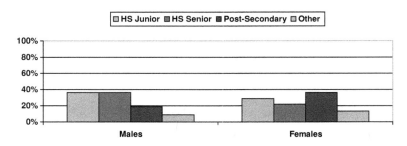

Figure 32. Comparing grade level percentage of male and female NT students.

Figure 33 compares males and females in NT programs based on residence. Fifty percent of both the male students and female students in the NT programs were from towns. There were more females from urban and suburban areas than males, but generally both males and females were living in town or rural areas.

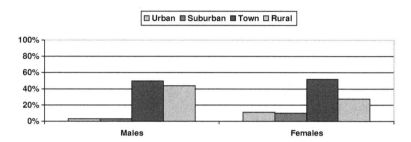

Figure 33. Comparing residence percentage of male and female NT students.

Comparative family incomes for males and females in NT programs are shown in Figure 34. Almost half of the females in the NT programs had family incomes of less than $10,000 and almost 25% were in the $30,000-$49,999. There were fewer NT females in the $10,000 and $30,000 range or above $50,000. More males were in the middle income range than in the lower or higher income ranges. More males were in the higher income brackets than females. Both male and female students were primarily living on less than $10,000 per year and this was especially true for females.

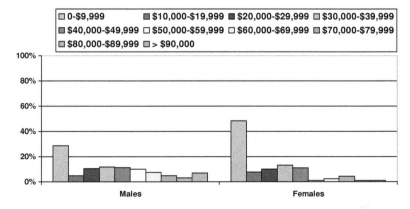

Figure 34. Comparing income percentage of male and female NT students.

Figure 35 reveals that the male students were 93% single. There were more single male NT students than females. There were more females that were married or divorced than males. There were few separated students and almost equal percentages for males and females. There were no males that were widowed. Both female and male students in the NT programs were mostly single.

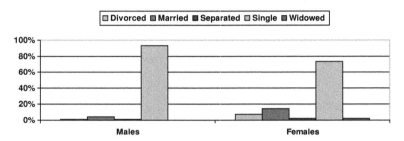

Figure 35. Comparing marital status percentage of male and female NT students.

Figure 36 shows that the males had more students with one sibling at home than females. Females had the highest percentage with no siblings and the percentage decreased as the number of siblings increased. Females had a higher percentage than males with three siblings.

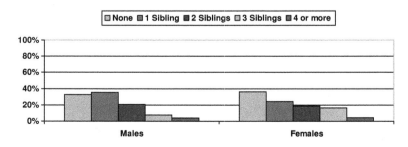

Figure 36. Comparing siblings at home percentage of male and female NT students.

Figure 37 and 38 compare parental employment in a technology field for males

and females in NT programs. As shown in Figure 37, the percentage of fathers working

in technology fields was almost the same for males and females. Generally, very few

fathers of the NT students worked in technology.

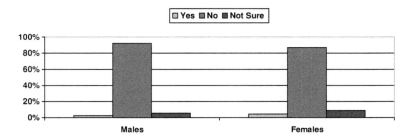

Figure 37. Comparing fathers in technology field percentage of male and female NT
students.

Figure 38 shows that the percent of mothers working in a technology field was

also far less than the percent of mothers not working in a technology field for both males

and females, but was slightly higher for male students.

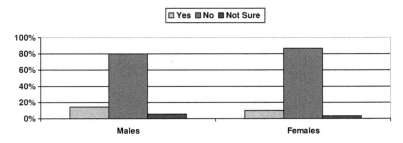

Figure 38. Comparing mothers in technology field percentage of male and female NT
students.

Parental employment in technology is summarized in Figure 39. While most NT

students of both genders did not have either parent working in technology, the percent of fathers working in a technology field was less than the percent of mothers working in a technology field for both males and females. The percentage of fathers and mothers working in technology was higher for male students than female students.

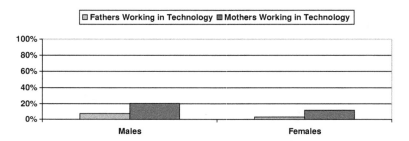

Figure 39. Comparing fathers and mothers working in a technology field percentage of male and female NT students.

As shown in Figure 40, ten percent more NT females received some form of assistance and career counseling than the males. Two of the females recorded comments reporting counseling through workforce and vocational rehabilitation. The three males that recorded a comment listed Education Enhancement Center, anger management, and the military. The majority of the students did not receive career counseling through assistance programs.

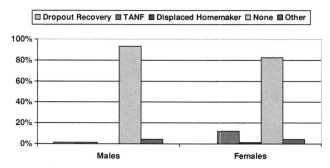

Figure 40. Comparing career counseling percentage of male and female NT students.

As shown in Figure 41, most males and females were admitted into their first choice of NT programs. There were 12 (13.2%) females not admitted into their first choice of programs. Those who posted a comment reported wanting medical administration, but were attending classes in the general accounting program. One student reported health science as their first choice and horticulture was their second choice, and another student wanted cosmetology, but was attending a section of the law enforcement program. The males reported more comments about not being admitted into their first choice of programs. One male student's first choice was radio broadcasting, but was in a culinary program. Another student listed diesel mechanic as his first choice and electrical as current program. Two male students that were admitted into the welding program reported that machine tools and auto paint/body were their first choices. Two students in law enforcement wanted welding and health science. Three students in the carpentry program listed auto technician, welding, and heat/air as first choices. However, the large majority of both males and females in the NT programs were admitted into their first choice program.

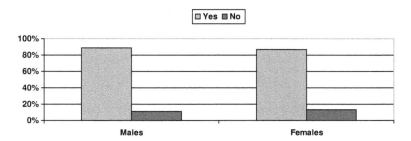

Figure 41. Comparing first choice percentage of male and female NT students.

As shown in Figure 42, more NT females reported experiencing a selection process than the NT male students. The females that recorded a comment in the comment section about the selection process reported there was an interview to enroll in health careers. One female commented that there was a test to be admitted into the culinary arts program. The males that commented said that there was an interview for the diesel mechanic program and a placement test for the welding program. Most of both gender groups did not have a selection process to be admitted into a NT program.

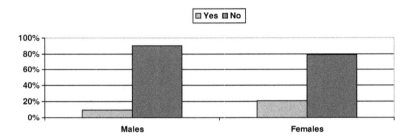

Figure 42. Comparing selection process percentage of male and female NT students.

Figure 43 reports the disabilities reported by males and females in NT programs. There were 26 (28.6%) of the females and 36 (14.3%) of the males in NT programs that reported a disability or disadvantage. There was a higher percentage for hearing disabilities, cognitively disadvantages, and academically disadvantaged for the females than for the males, but males had a higher percentage than females with impaired vision, impaired motor development, and were economically disadvantaged. Females had the highest percentage of students that were academically disadvantaged (n=12, 15.2%). Males had the highest percentage of students that were economically disadvantaged (n=12, 7.5%). Both male and female NT students generally reported no disabilities or disadvantages.

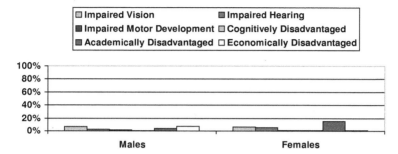

Figure 43. Comparing disabilities percentage of male and female NT students.

Summary of Demographics Profiles Comparing Males and Females in NT Programs

The males and females in NT programs were mainly young, Caucasian, and single. The males were mainly in high school while the females were mainly Post-Secondary. The male student profile for location of residency was similar to the profile of the female CT students. There were a substantially larger percent of females than males in the lowest income level, but both were largely living in the poorest income level.

Scarcely any of males or females had four or more siblings at home, parents working in technology, or counseling through assistance programs before choosing a CareerTech program. Most of both gender groups entered a program of their choosing without a selection process. Few students of either gender reported a disability or disadvantage, but there were more females reporting academic disadvantages than males and more males reporting more economic disadvantages than females in NT programs.

Demographics Profiles Comparing Males and Females in CT and NT Programs

The sample of 424 was divided into two groups according to their career choice. There were 173 students identified as part of a program that were training for a computer technology career. Of those 173 students, there were 134 females and 39 males. There

119

were 251 students enrolled in programs that did not focus on a computer technology career. There were 91 females and 160 males. The four groups from the sample are identified as CT males, CT females, NT males, and NT females.

The NT males were the youngest and the CT females were the oldest. Figure 44 shows the age groups distribution for both genders in both program groups. The CT females were more evenly dispersed that the other three groups. The CT males and NT females were somewhat similar in age distribution with more than half under the age of 20. The CT males were mostly young but had the oldest student at the age of 88.

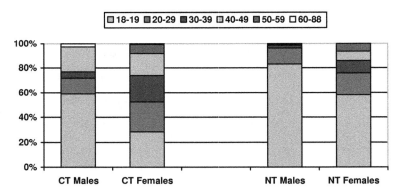

Figure 44. Comparing age percentages of CT males and females and NT males and females.

As shown in Figure 45, the CT males had the smallest percentage of Caucasian students and the NT males had the largest percentage. However, the percentage of Caucasian males was almost equal for CT and NT. The CT females had the smallest percentage of African Americans and the NT females had the highest percentage of African Americans. The CT males and female Native Americans students were about equal. The NT males and females were about equal, but about 10% less than the male and

120

female CT students. There were more Hispanic NT males than NT females, CT males, or CT females.

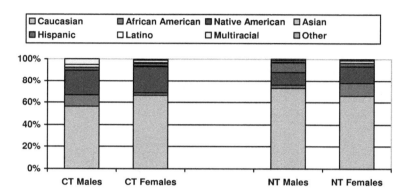

Figure 45. Comparing race percentages of male NT and CT and female NT and CT.

Figure 46 shows that the NT females and CT males were almost equally divided between high school and post-secondary students. The CT females were mostly post-secondary, and NT males were mostly high school students.

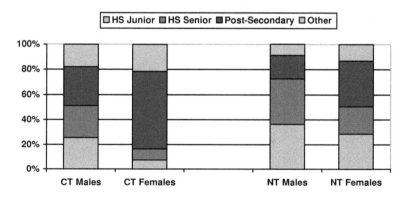

Figure 46. Comparing grade level percentages of male NT and CT and female NT and CT.

The sample was heavily weighted with representatives from town and rural locations; it contained very few students from urban and suburban locations. As shown in Figure 47, there were no students from the urban or suburban areas in the CT male section and only one in the CT female section. The NT females had the highest percentage of urban and suburban students. The CT males had a higher percentage of students that were living in towns, and the CT females had the highest percentage from rural areas.

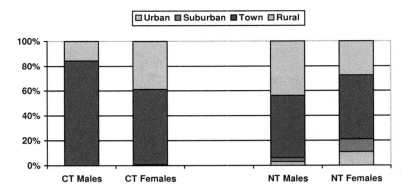

Figure 47. Comparing residence percentages of male NT and CT and female NT and CT.

Income distributions are shown in Figure 48. The NT males had a smaller percentage of students living in a house hold of less than $10,000 and a larger percentage of students in the higher income ranges than the NT females, CT males, or CT females. The NT males were more evenly distributed among the different income brackets.

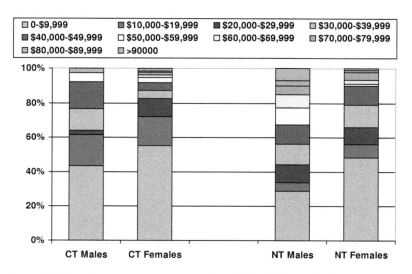

Figure 48. Comparing income percentages of male NT and CT and female NT and CT.

The sample comprised largely single students. However, as shown in Figure 49, the CT females had fewer percentages of single students and more married students than the other three groups. The NT males had higher percentages of single students and fewer married students than the other three groups. The NT females and the CT males were similar in distribution of the marital status of their students, which was primarily single but almost equal number of students that were married, divorced, and widowed.

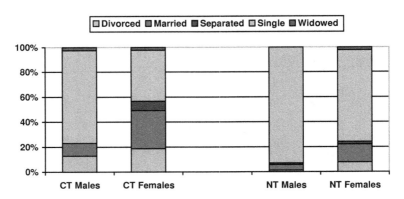

Figure 49. Comparing marital percentages of male NT and CT and female NT and CT.

As shown in Figure 50, the CT males had a larger percentage with no siblings at home and the largest percentage with one sibling at home. All groups consistently had a lesser percentage as the number of siblings increased from zero to four or more, except the CT females. There were almost 1.5% more students with four or more than with three siblings.

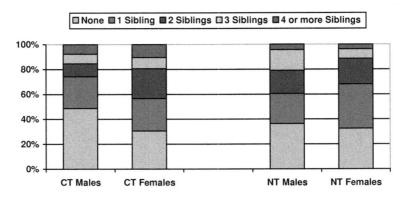

Figure 50. Comparing sibling percentages of male NT and CT and female NT and CT.

Figures 51 and 52 summarize the findings related to having a parent working in a technology field. Both Figures clearly indicate that no group had many parents employed in technology. As shown in Figure 51, a higher percent of CT males had fathers working in a technology field than other groups.

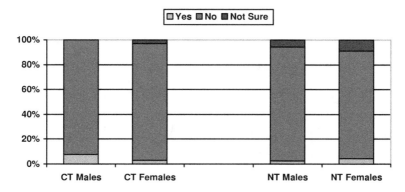

Figure 51. Comparing father in technology field percentages of male NT and CT and female NT and CT.

Figure 52 also shows that the CT males also had the highest percentage of mothers working in a technology field.

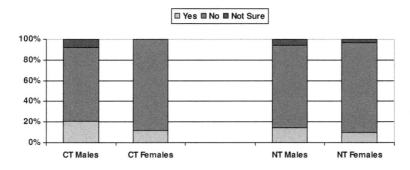

Figure 52. Comparing mother in technology field percentages of male NT and CT and female NT and CT.

Figure 53 shows the data related to assistance programs and career counseling for all groups. The CT females received more specified career counseling and assistance than the other groups. Both females groups received more formal career counseling required through programs than both male groups. Only two students were in the dropout recovery program and they were both males in NT programs.

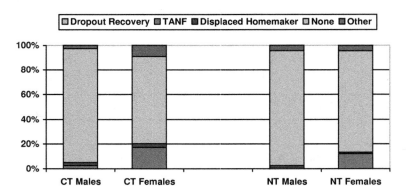

Figure 53. Comparing career counseling percentages of male NT and CT and female NT and CT.

As shown in Figure 54, about 87-88% of all groups were able to enter the program of choice. The CT males had a some what higher percentage at 97.4%. Only one student (2.6%) was unable to enroll in the program of choice.

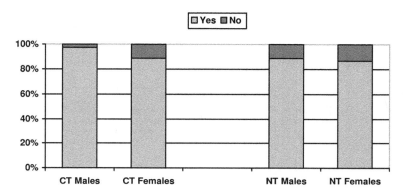

Figure 54. Comparing first choice percentages of male NT and CT and female NT and CT.

Figure 55 shows that about 20% of both female groups experienced a selection process to enroll in their choice of program, while only about 10% of both male groups were required to meet requirements in a selection process.

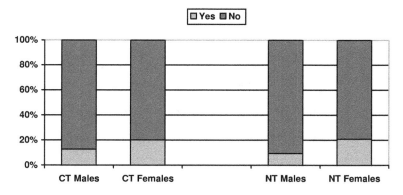

Figure 55. Comparing selection process percentages of male NT and CT and female NT and CT.

Figure 56 presents the disability and disadvantage profiles for all groups. The groups do not represent 100% because not all students reported a disability or disadvantage.

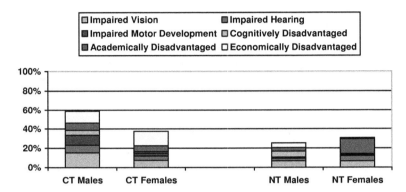

Figure 56. Comparing disabilities percentages of male NT and CT and female NT and CT.

Summary of Demographical Profiles Comparing Males and Females in CT and NT Programs

All four groups were similar is distribution for ethnicity (primarily Caucasian), number of siblings at home (less than three), and fathers and mothers working in a technology field. The four groups were similar in the overall appearance of the distribution of the assistance and career counseling (most did not receive), being admitted into the program of choice (most were), and having to go through a selection process to be admitted into the program of choice (most did not). Very few students from the metro campuses participated in the study and very few from any of the four groups listed urban or suburban as their residence. The distribution for rural, town, suburban, and urban was about the same for all four groups.

The CT males reported more disadvantages and disabilities that the other three groups with over half of the students reporting a disability or disadvantage. The NT males were more evenly spread from the lowest income level to the highest income level than the other three groups. The greatest concentration pf income below $10,000 was in the females, particularly the CT females. The range of student ages varied more for the CT females than the other three groups. The CT females also were different from the other three groups in that the majority of the students were post-secondary and not as many were single.

Research Question Three:

What is the profile of influences and barriers for students who pursue careers in computer technology and how does it compare with non-technology careers?

Responses from survey questions 17-60 were used to answer research questions three and four. Survey questions 17-28 were part of the historical part of the survey and required a response of how often students used technology, including computers, cell phones, computer games, and opportunities to use computers. Response was made on a 5-point Likert scale where one was never, two was rarely, three was sometimes, four was often, and five was very often. Using this 5-point Likert scale, two levels of response were formed. Using 1-3 of the scale, a grouped titled "Low Use" was created. Likert points 4-5 were grouped to form a group titled "High Use".

Survey questions 29-40 required a response of agreement or non-agreement to questions about the use of and opinions about technology. Survey questions 29-40 used a 5-point Likert scale that asked if the students agreed or disagreed with the statement, where one was strongly disagree, two was disagree, three was neutral, four was agree, and five was strongly agree. The students that selected a one, two, or three were categorized as "Neutral or Disagree" and those that selected a four or five were placed in the category titled "Agree".

The third section of the survey contained a list of people that might have had some influence on the students' career decisions. Survey questions 41-60 required a response of agreement or non-agreement, if applicable, in reference to influences from people those responses using a 6-point Likert scale (0-5), where zero was not applicable, one was very negative, two was somewhat negative, three was neutral, four was somewhat positive, and five was very positive. Students who selected zero were put in a group titled "Not Applicable" while students that selected one or two were grouped together and titled "Negative". Students that selected three were placed in a group titled "Neutral" while students that selected four or five were grouped together and titled "Positive".

Influences and Barriers Profiles Comparing CT and NT Students

The responses to the survey questions 17-60 were divided into two groups, either CT or NT, according to the program they were attending at the Oklahoma CareerTech. The student responses were used to answer research question number three. Table 14 contains responses for survey questions 17-28 (Technology Use and Opportunities) for CT and NT students.

Table 14

Frequencies and Percentages of Technology Use and Opportunities for CT and NT Students for Survey Questions 17-28

Technology Use[a]		
	CT Students (n=173)	NT Students (n=251)

	Low Use[b]	High Use[c]	Low Use	High Use
Q17 Used computers in elementary school	145 (83.8%)	28 (16.2%)	184 (73.3%)	67 (26.7%)
Q18 Used computers in middle school	118 (68.2%)	55 (31.8%)	153 (61.0%)	98 (39.0%)
Q19 Used computers in high school	88 (50.9%)	85 (49.1%)	99 (39.4%)	152 (60.6%)
Q20 Used computers at home during elementary school	156 (90.2%)	17 (09.8%)	224 (89.2%)	27 (10.8%)
Q21 Used computers at home during middle school	135 (78.0%)	38 (22.0%)	189 (75.3%)	62 (24.7%)
Q22 Used computers at home during high school	110 (63.6%)	63 (36.4%)	138 (55.0%)	113 (45.0%)
Q23 Currently have a computer at home	59 (34.1%)	114 (65.9%)	71 (28.3%0	180 (71.7%)
Q24 Currently use a cell phone	76 (43.9%)	97 (56.1%)	92 (36.7%)	159 (63.3%)
Q25 Played computer games as a child	115 (66.5%)	58 (33.5%)	121 (48.2%)	130 (51.8%)
Q26 Currently play computer games	136 (78.6%)	37 (21.4%)	148 (59.0%)	103 (41.0%)
Q27 Have opportunities to use new technologies	80 (46.2%)	93 (53.8%)	151 (60.2%)	100 (39.8%)
Q28 Have opportunities to learn new technologies	60 (34.7%)	113 (65.3%)	130 (51.8%)	121 (48.2%)

[a]Rounding errors may have prevented percentages from equaling 100%.
[b]Using 1-3 of Likert Scale.
[c]Using 4-5 of Likert Scale.

Survey questions 17-28 revealed that neither CT nor NT students had much use with computers in elementary or middle school. More students used computers in middle school than elementary school, but still less than 40% used computers in middle school. However, 60.6% of NT students and 49.1% of CT students used computers in high school. Since use of computers in schools has increased over the past ten years, it seems reasonable that more students used computers in high school rather than elementary school. Less than half of the students used computers at home during any of the three levels of school. Students did use computers at home increasingly more from elementary to high school years in both groups. The NT students used computers in school approximately 10% more than the CT students in all three levels of school. They also used computers at home during their school years more than the CT students, but only 1% more during elementary school, less than 3% more during middle school, and 8% more during high school. Both groups had high use of computers at home at the present time, with the NT students being slightly more.

Both groups also had a larger percentage of students that currently used cell phones than those that did not use cell phones. The NT students currently use cell phones 7% more than CT students. Less than a third of the CT students played computerized games as a child while a little more than half of the NT students played computer games as a child. Even fewer currently played computer games, with both groups having less than half reporting they did play computerized games, but there were still more NT than CT students that played computer games.

The NT students had a larger percentage than CT students of "high use" of technology in school, at home, with cell phones, and computer games. The only area that CT students had larger percentages than the NT students were questions 27 and 28 that referred to opportunities to use or learn new technologies. Computer technology students reported that over half had high levels of opportunities to *use* new technologies while less than 40% of NT students had the same opportunities. Similarly, over 65% of the CT students had high levels of opportunity to *learn* new technologies while only 48.2% of NT students reported such opportunities.

Survey questions 29 - 40 required a response of agreement or disagreement about

technology perceptions, discrimination, and influences. The frequencies and percentages

are shown in Table 15.

Table 15

Frequencies and Percentages of Influences and Barriers for CT and NT Programs for Survey Questions 29-40

Influences and Barriers[a]				
	CT Students (n=173)		NT Students (n=251)	
	Neutral or Disagree[b]	Agree[c]	Neutral or Disagree	Agree
Q29 Negative images influenced career decisions	166 (96.0%)	7 (4.0%)	227 (90.4%)	24 (9.6%)
Q30 Perceived working conditions influenced career decisions	86 (49.7%)	87 (50.3%)	214 (85.3%)	37 (14.7%)
Q31 Derogatory comments about Technology	154 (89.0%)	19 (11.0%)	218 (86.9%)	33 (13.1%)
Q32 Discriminate because of gender	153 (88.4%)	20 (11.6%)	217 (86.5%)	34 (13.5%)
Q33 Students are more productive because of technology	31 (17.9%)	142 (82.1%)	86 (34.3%)	165 (65.7%)
Q34 Technology is demoralizing	144 (83.2%)	29 (16.8%)	168 (66.9%)	83 (33.1%)
Q35 Computers simplify gathering data	31 (17.9%)	142 (82.1%)	75 (29.9%)	176 (70.1%)
Q36 Comfortable with using computers	11 (6.4%)	162 (93.6%)	72 (28.7%)	179 (71.3%)
Q37 Prefer printed materials	136 (78.6%)	37 (21.4%)	188 (74.9%)	63 (25.1%)
Q38 Computers are more trouble than worth	155 (89.6%)	18 (10.4%)	190 (75.7%)	61 (24.3%)
Q39 Schools spend too much on computers	162 (93.6%)	11 (6.4%)	207 (82.5%)	44 (17.5%)
Q40 Technology frees people from tedious work	79 (45.7%)	94 (54.3%)	135 (53.8%)	116 (46.2%)

[a] Rounding errors may have prevented percentages from equaling 100%.
[b]Using 1-3 of Likert Scale.
[c]Using 4-5 of Likert Scale.

133

A summary of survey questions 29-40 for CT and NT programs revealed that very few in either group believed that negative images about computer scientists influenced their career decisions. However, the percentage of NT students was over twice as many as CT students that did agree that negative images influenced their career decisions. The NT students had a higher percentage of students than CT students that experienced discrimination, were influenced by derogatory comments, thought computers were more trouble than they were worth, and preferred printed materials. However, the majority of both groups did not report being influenced by negative perceptions about or experiences with technology in their career decisions. Neither group reported gender discrimination as a major influence in choosing a CT or NT career.

Over half of the CT students thought that perceived working conditions about computer jobs influenced their career decisions compared to less than 15% of the NT students. Almost 30% did report that perceived working conditions influenced their career decisions. Only about 12% reported that derogatory comments about technology affected career decisions and only 8.5% had perceived some level of discrimination because of gender. About half of both groups thought that technology frees people from tedious work.

The data related to survey questions 41 - 60 for CT students are shown in Table 16 and data for NT students are shown in Table 17. The response categories were negative, positive, neutral, or not applicable about people that may have had an influence on career decisions.

Table 16

Frequencies and Percentages of Influences by People for CT Programs for Survey Questions 41-60

	People of Influence[a]			
	CT Students (n=173)			
	Not Applicable	Negative[b]	Neutral[c]	Positive[d]
Q41 Influenced by mother	18 (10.4%)	10 (5.8%)	23 (13.3%)	122 (70.5%)
Q42 Influenced by father	41 (23.7%)	13 (7.5%)	32 (18.5%)	87 (50.3%)
Q43 Influenced by sister	69 (39.9%)	9 (5.2%)	30 (17.3%)	65 (37.6%)
Q44 Influenced by brother	62 (35.8%)	15 (8.7%)	42 (24.3%)	54 (31.2%)
Q45 Influenced by children	74 (42.8%)	2 (1.2%)	16 (9.2%)	81 (46.8%)
Q46 Influenced by spouse	77 (44.5%)	8 (4.6%)	18 (10.4%)	70 (40.5%)
Q47 Influenced by other family members	22 (12.7%)	4 (2.3%)	41 (23.7%)	106 (61.3%)
Q48 Influenced by friends	15 (8.7%)	1 (0.6%)	32 (18.5%)	125 (72.3%)
Q49 Influenced by elementary school teachers	67 (38.7%)	11 (6.4%)	46 (26.6%)	49 (28.3%)
Q50 Influenced by middle school technology teachers	73 (42.2%)	9 (5.2%)	37 (21.4%)	54 (31.2%)
Q51 Influenced by high school technology teachers	62 (35.8%)	5 (2.9%)	33 (19.1%)	73 (42.2%)
Q52 Influenced by other teachers	59 (34.1%)	5 (2.9%)	42 (24.3%)	67 (38.7%)
Q53 Influenced by guidance counselors	48 (27.7%)	8 (4.6%)	32 (18.5%)	85 (49.1%)
Q54 Influenced by female high school classmates	52 (30.1%)	7 (4.0%)	50 (28.9%)	64 (37.0%)
Q55 Influenced by male high school classmates	56 (32.4%)	13 (7.5%)	61 (35.3%)	43 (24.9%)
Q56 Influenced by supervisors at work	72 (41.6%)	7 (4.0%)	27 (15.6%)	67 (38.7%)
Q57 Influenced by co-workers	70 (40.5%)	2 (1.2%)	31 (17.9%)	70 (40.5%)
Q58 Influenced by public figures	76 (43.9%)	5 (2.9%)	29 (16.8%)	63 (36.4%)
Q59 Influenced by fictional characters	87 (50.3%)	7 (4.0%)	43 (24.9%)	36 (20.8%)
Q60 Influenced by others	84 (48.6%)	4 (2.3%)	19 (11.0%)	66 (38.2%)

[a]Rounding errors may have prevented percentages from equaling 100%.
[b]Using 1-2 of Likert Scale.
[c]Using 3 of Likert Scale.
[d]Using 4-5 of Likert Scale.

Table 17

Frequencies and Percentages of Influences by People for NT Programs for Survey Questions 41-60

	People of Influence[a]			
	NT Students (n=251)			
	Not Applicable	[b]Negative	[c]Neutral	[d]Positive
Q41 Influenced by mother	19 (7.6%)	23 (9.2%)	50 (19.9%)	159 (63.3%)
Q42 Influenced by father	36 (14.3%)	23 (9.2%)	49 (19.5%)	143 (57.0%)
Q43 Influenced by sister	85 (33.9%)	16 (6.4%)	63 (25.1%)	87 (34.7%)
Q44 Influenced by brother	67 (26.7%)	16 (6.4%)	75 (29.9%)	93 (37.1%)
Q45 Influenced by children	193 (76.9%)	3 (1.2%)	22 (8.8%)	33 (13.1%)
Q46 Influenced by spouse	155 (61.8%)	11 (4.4%)	16 (6.4%)	69 (27.5%)
Q47 Influenced by other family members	19 (7.6%)	20 (8.0%)	62 (24.7%)	150 (59.8%)
Q48 Influenced by friends	14 (5.6%)	14 (5.6%)	63 (25.1%)	160 (63.7%)
Q49 Influenced by elementary school teachers	74 (29.5%)	13 (5.2%)	69 (27.5%)	95 (37.8%)
Q50 Influenced by middle school technology teachers	71 (28.3%)	18 (7.2%)	74 (29.5%)	88 (35.1%)
Q51 Influenced by high school technology teachers	47 (18.7%)	18 (7.2%)	51 (20.3%)	135 (53.8%)
Q52 Influenced by other teachers	57 (22.7%)	13 (5.2%)	65 (25.9%)	116 (46.2%)
Q53 Influenced by guidance counselors	49 (19.5%)	18 (7.2%)	61 (24.3%)	123 (49.0%)
Q54 Influenced by female high school classmates	38 (15.1%)	19 (7.6%)	81 (32.3%)	113 (45.0%)
Q55 Influenced by male high school classmates	39 (15.5%)	39 (15.5%)	83 (33.1%)	90 (35.9%)
Q56 Influenced by supervisors at work	75 (29.9%)	19 (7.6%)	65 (25.9%)	92 (36.7%)
Q57 Influenced by co-workers	77 (30.7%)	16 (6.4%)	72 (28.7%)	86 (34.3%)
Q58 Influenced by public figures	74 (29.5%)	18 (7.2%)	91 (36.3%)	68 (27.1%)
Q59 Influenced by fictional characters	89 (35.5%)	15 (6.0%)	95 (37.8%)	52 (20.7%)
Q60 Influenced by others	88 (35.1%)	7 (2.8%)	73 (29.1%)	83 (33.1%)

[a] Rounding errors may have prevented percentages from equaling 100%.
[b] Using 1-2 of Likert Scale.
[c] Using 3 of Likert Scale.
[d] Using 4-5 of Likert Scale.

An examination of survey questions 41-60 for CT and NT students revealed that the majority of both groups were positively influenced in their career decisions by family. The positive percentages were much higher than the negative percentages is every category. Friends had the highest percentage of positive influence than any other category for both CT and NT students.

Computer technology students reported higher percentages of positive influence from children and spouses, but they had a larger percentage of older married students than the NT students. Female family members were more influential for CT students and male family members were more influential for NT students. The highest percentage of students that were positively influenced by their mothers was the CT students. The highest percentage of students negatively influenced was equal between mothers and fathers of NT students. The highest percentage of students in the CT programs that were negatively influenced was by brothers.

High school technology teachers had larger percentages provide a positive influence than other high school teachers or elementary and middle school teachers. Non-technology students were influenced more by both male and females that CT students. Public figures and fictional characters were not important influences on career decisions for either CT or NT students.

Summary of Influences and Barriers Profiles Comparing CT and NT Students

Students that have opportunities to use and learn new technologies are the students who selected CT programs, but students that were exposed to computers in school and home during their childhood are not in CT programs. More NT students currently have cell phones and computers than the CT students.

Only a small percent of students in either group reported that negative perceptions, derogatory comments, and gender discrimination had an influence on their career decision. However, 50% of the CT students reported that perceived working conditions influenced career decisions. More CT than NT students believed that computers simplified gathering data, increased productivity, and were comfortable with computers. More NT than CT students believed that computers demoralizing, more trouble than they were worth, and schools spent too much money on computers. Both CT and NT students were almost equally split between whether technology freed people from tedious work.

Family, friends, teachers, counselors, classmates, co-workers, and others, all had a more positive influence than negative influence on both CT and NT students. Friends and mothers had the highest percents of positive influence on both groups. Non-technology students were positively influenced by high school technology teachers more than CT students. Both CT and NT students were positively influenced more by high school technology teachers than by other high school teachers, middle schools teachers, or elementary teachers. However high school counselors had a higher percentage (49.1%) than even the high school technology teachers for CT students. There was very little impact from public figures and fictional characters on either group.

Research Question Four:

Are those influences and barriers profiles the same for male and female students?

Responses from survey questions 17-60 from CT and NT students were divided according to gender. Responses are compiled in Tables 18-25. Table 18 shows student responses to questions 17-28 for male and female CT students and Table 19 shows

138

student responses to questions 17-28 for male and female NT students. Table 20 shows

student responses to questions 29-40 for male and female CT students and Table 21

shows student responses to questions 29-40 for male and female NT students. Table 22

reports data for CT female students, Table 23 reports data for CT males, Table 24 reports

data for NT females, and Table 25 reports data for NT males from survey questions 41-

60.

Influences and Barriers Profiles Comparing Male and Female Students in CT and NT

Programs

Data related to survey questions 17 - 28 for CT students is in Table 18 and data

for NT students is in Table 19.

Table 18

*Frequencies and Percentages of Technology Use and Opportunities for Females and
Males in CT Programs for Survey Questions 17-28*

Technology Use for Students in CT Programs[a]				
	Females (n=134)		Males (n=39)	
	Low Use[b]	High Use[c]	Low Use	High Use
Q17 Used computers in elementary school	116 (86.6%)	18 (13.4%)	29 (74.4%)	10 (25.6%)
Q18 Used computers in middle school	95 (70.9%)	39 (29.1%)	23 (59.0%)	16 (41.0%)
Q19 Used computers in high school	72 (53.7%)	62 (46.3%)	16 (41.0%)	23 (59.0%)
Q20 Used computers at home during elementary school	112 (83.6%)	12 (9.0%)	34 (87.2%)	5 (12.8%)
Q21 Used computers at home during middle school	109 (81.3%)	25 (18.7%)	26 (66.7%)	13 (33.3%)
Q22 Used computers at home during high school	92 (68.7%)	42 (31.3%)	18 (46.2%)	21 (53.8%)
Q23 Currently have a computer at home	51 (38.1%)	83 (61.9%)	8 (20.5%)	31 (79.5%)
Q24 Currently use a cell phone	52 (38.8%)	82 (61.2%)	24 (61.5%)	15 (38.5%)

Q25 Played computer games as a child	97 (72.4%)	37 (27.6%)	18 (46.2%)	21 (53.8%)
Q26 Currently play computer games	118 (88.1%)	16 (11.9%)	18 (46.2%)	21 (53.8%)
Q27 Have opportunities to use new technologies	62 (46.3%)	72 (53.7%)	18 (46.2%)	21 (53.8%)
Q28 Have opportunities to learn new technologies	47 (35.1%)	87 (64.9%)	13 (33.3%)	26 (66.7%)

[a]Rounding errors may have prevented percentages from equaling 100%.
[b]Using 1-3 of Likert Scale.
[c]Using 4-5 of Likert Scale.

A comparison of males and females in CT programs revealed that the percent increased with computer use as students move from elementary to middle school and high school. The percentages also increased for males and females that used computers at home while in school as they became older and graduated to middle school and high school, but was more for males than females in every category.

More CT males currently have computers at home, played computer games as a child, and more currently play computer games. However, more CT females have high use of cell phones than CT males. Females and males were almost equal in having opportunities to *learn* and *use* new technology. Both groups had approximately 54% that had opportunities to *use* new technologies and approximately 65% that had opportunities to *learn* new technologies.

Table 19

Frequencies and Percentages for Technology Use and Opportunities Profiles for Females and Males in NT Programs for Survey Questions 17-28

Technology Use for Students in NT Programs[a]				
	Females (n=91)		Males (n=160)	
	Low Use[b]	High Use[c]	Low Use	High Use
Q17 Used computers in elementary school	69 (75.8%)	22 (24.2%)	115 (71.9%)	45 (28.1%)

Q18 Used computers in middle school	59 (64.8%)	32 (35.2%)	94 (58.8%)	66 (41.3%)
Q19 Used computers in high school	36 (39.6%)	55 (60.4%)	63 (39.4%)	97 (60.6%)
Q20 Used computers at home during elementary school	81 (89.0%)	10 (11.0%)	143 (89.4%)	17 (10.6%)
Q21Used computers at home during middle school	71 (78.0%)	20 (22.0%)	118 (73.8%)	42 (26.3%)
Q22Used computers at home during high school	40 (44.0%)	51 (56.0%)	98 (61.3%)	62 (38.8%)
Q23 Currently have a computer at home	32 (35.2%)	59 (64.8%)	39 (24.4%)	121 (75.6%)
Q24 Currently use a cell phone	28 (30.8%)	63 (69.2%)	64 (40.0%)	96 (60.0%)
Q25 Played computer games as a child	54 (59.3%)	37 (40.7%)	67 (41.9%)	93 (58.1%)
Q26 Currently play computer games	51 (56.0%)	40 (44.0%)	97 (60.6%)	63 (39.4%)
Q27 Have opportunities to use new technologies	46 (50.5%)	45 (49.5%)	105 (65.6%)	55 (34.4%)
Q28 Have opportunities to learn new technologies	57 (62.6%)	34 (37.4%)	73 (45.6%)	87 (54.4%)

[a]Rounding errors may have prevented percentages from equaling 100%.
[b]Using 1-3 of Likert Scale.
[c]Using 4-5 of Likert Scale.

A comparison of males and females in a NT program from questions 17-28 revealed that the use of computers increased as students move from elementary to high school. However, there were considerably more NT females than NT males that used computers at home during their high school years, which is different from the CT students.

More NT males currently have computers at home than NT females. As with the CT females, more females have cell phones than NT males. More males played computer games as a child, but more NT females currently play computer games than NT males. There are more females that currently play computer games than did as a child. There were more NT females that have opportunities to *use* new technologies, but more NT

males with the opportunity to *learn* new technologies.

The data related to survey questions 29 - 40 are shown in Tables 20 for female

and male CT students and Table 21 for female and male NT students.

Table 20

Frequencies and Percentages of Influences and Barriers Profiles for Females and Males in CT Programs for Survey Questions 29-40

Influences and Barriers for CT Programs[a]				
	Females (n=134)		Males (n=39)	
	Neutral or Disagree[b]	Agree[c]	Neutral or Disagree	Agree
Q29 Negative images influenced career decisions	129 (96.3%)	5 (3.7%)	37 (94.9%)	2 (5.1%)
Q30 Perceived working conditions influenced career decisions	72 (53.7%)	62 (46.3%)	14 (35.9%)	25 (64.1%)
Q31 Derogatory comments about Technology	122 (91.0%)	12 (9.0%)	32 (82.1%)	7 (17.9%)
Q32 Discriminate because of gender	118 (88.1%)	16 (11.9%)	35 (89.7%)	4 (10.3%)
Q33 Students are more productive because of technology	18 (13.4%)	116 (86.6%)	13 (33.3%)	26 (66.7%)
Q34 Technology is demoralizing	117 (87.3%)	17 (12.7%)	27 (69.2%)	12 (30.8%)
Q35 Computers simplify gathering data	24 (17.9%)	110 (82.1%)	7 (17.9%)	32 (82.1%)
Q36 Comfortable with using computers	8 (6.0%)	126 (94.0%)	3 (7.7%)	36 (92.3%)
Q37 Prefer printed materials	105 (78.4%)	29 (21.6%)	31 (79.5%)	8 (20.5%)
Q38 Computers are more trouble than worth	119 (88.8%)	15 (11.2%)	36 (92.3%)	3 (7.7%)
Q39 Schools spend too much on computers	129 (96.3%)	5 (3.7%)	33 (84.6%)	6 (15.4%)
Q40 Technology frees people from tedious work	61 (45.5%)	73 (54.5%)	18 (46.2%)	21 (53.8%)

[a]Rounding errors may have prevented percentages from equaling 100%.
[b]Using 1-3 of Likert Scale.
[c]Using 4-5 of Likert Scale.

A summary of questions 29-40 for males and females in CT programs revealed that very few in either group believed that negative images about computer scientists influenced their career decisions. The CT male students had a higher percentage than female students that were influenced by derogatory comments, preconceived working conditions, thought that technology was demoralizing, and that schools spend too much money on computers, but there were very few in either group. Only about 20% of both males and females preferred the printed materials and about half of both groups thought that technology frees people from tedious work. Both CT females and males agreed that they were influenced be perceived working conditions of computer jobs. Most categories were somewhat equal in comparison between females and males. There were approximately 20% more CT females than CT males that thought students were more productive because of technology. Almost 95% of both groups were comfortable with computers.

Table 21

Frequencies and Percentages of Influences and Barriers Profiles for Males and Females in NT Programs for Survey Questions 29-40

Influences and Barriers for NT Programs[a]				
	Females (n=91)		Males (n=160)	
	Neutral or Disagree[b]	Agree[c]	Neutral or Disagree	Agree
Q29 Negative images influenced career decisions	82 (90.1%)	9 (9.9%)	145 (90.6%)	15 (9.4%)
Q30 Perceived working conditions influenced career decisions	75 (82.4%)	16 (17.6%)	139 (86.9%)	21 (13.1%)
Q31 Derogatory comments about Technology	79 (86.8%)	12 (13.2%)	139 (86.9%)	21 (13.1%)
Q32 Discriminate because of gender	78 (85.7%)	13 (14.3%)	139 (86.9%)	21 (13.1%)
Q33 Students are more	28 (30.8%)	63 (69.2%)	58 (36.3%)	102 (63.8%)

	Not Applicable	Negative[b]	Neutral[c]	Positive[d]
productive because of technology				
Q34 Technology is demoralizing	59 (64.8%)	32 (35.2%)	109 (68.1%)	51 (31.9%)
Q35 Computers simplify gathering data	26 (28.6%)	65 (71.4%)	49 (30.6%)	111 (69.4%)
Q36 Comfortable with using computers	25 (27.5%)	66 (72.5%)	47 (29.4%)	113 (70.6%)
Q37 Prefer printed materials	71 (78.0%)	20 (22.0%)	117 (73.1%)	43 (26.9%)
Q38 Computers are more trouble than worth	68 (74.7%)	23 (25.3%)	122 (76.3%)	38 (23.8%)
Q39 Schools spend too much on computers	77 (84.6%)	14 (15.4%)	130 (81.3%)	30 (18.8%)
Q40 Technology frees people from tedious work	52 (57.1%)	39 (42.9%)	83 (51.9%)	77 (48.1%)

[a]Rounding errors may have prevented percentages from equaling 100%.
[b]Using 1-3 of Likert Scale.
[c]Using 4 -5 of Likert Scale.

A comparison of questions 29-40 for males and females in NT programs revealed

that less than 10% of either group believed that negative images about computer

scientists influenced their career decisions. The males and females were within 5% of

each other on all of the survey questions.

The data related to survey questions 41 - 60 for females and males in CT

programs are shown in Tables 22 and 23.

Table 22

Frequencies and Percentages of Influences and Barriers Profiles for Females in CT Programs for Survey Questions 41-60

People of Influence			
Females in CT[a] (n=134)			
	Not Applicable	Negative[b]	Neutral[c]	Positive[d]
Q41 Influenced by mother	15 (11.2%)	8 (6.0%)	18 (13.4%)	93 (69.4%)
Q42 Influenced by father	36 (26.9%)	10 (7.5%)	22 (16.4%)	66 (49.3%)
Q43 Influenced by sister	51 (38.1%)	7 (5.2%)	21 (15.7%)	55 (41.0%)
Q44 Influenced by brother	48 (35.8%)	11 (8.2%)	31 (23.1%)	44 (32.8%)

Q45 Influenced by children	50 (37.3%)	1 (0.7%)	11 (8.2%)	72 (53.7%)
Q46 Influenced by spouse	56 (41.8%)	6 (4.5%)	13 (9.7%)	59 (44.0%)
Q47 Influenced by other family members	16 (11.9%)	2 (1.5%)	29 (21.6%)	87 (64.9%)
Q48 Influenced by friends	8 (6.0%)	0 (0.0%)	23 (17.2%)	103 (76.9%)
Q49 Influenced by elementary school teachers	57 (42.5%)	5 (3.7%)	30 (22.4%)	42 (31.3%)
Q50 Influenced by middle school technology teachers	62 (46.3%)	5 (3.7%)	27 (20.1%)	40 (29.9%)
Q51 Influenced by high school technology teachers	52 (38.8%)	3 (2.2%)	22 (16.4%)	57 (42.5%)
Q52 Influenced by other teachers	48 (35.8%)	3 (2.2%)	28 (20.9%)	55 (41.0%)
Q53 Influenced by guidance counselors	37 (27.6%)	6 (4.5%)	22 (16.4%)	69 (51.5%)
Q54 Influenced by female high school classmates	42 (31.3%)	5 (3.7%)	38 (28.4%)	49 (36.6%)
Q55 Influenced by male high school classmates	46 (34.3%)	9 (6.7%)	47 (35.1%)	32 (23.9%)
Q56 Influenced by supervisors at work	55 (41.0%)	4 (3.0%)	16 (11.9%)	59 (44.0%)
Q57 Influenced by co-workers	52 (38.8%)	0 (0.0%)	24 (17.9%)	58 (43.3%)
Q58 Influenced by public figures	37 (27.6%)	5 (3.7%)	29 (21.6%)	63 (47.0%)
Q59 Influenced by fictional characters	48 (35.8%)	7 (5.2%)	43 (32.1%)	36 (26.9%)
Q60 Influenced by others	45 (33.6%)	4 (3.0%)	19 (14.2%)	66 (49.3%)

[a]Rounding errors may have prevented percentages from equaling 100%.
[b]Using 1-2 of Likert Scale.
[c]Using 3 of Likert Scale.
[d]Using 4-5 of Likert Scale.

Table 23

Frequencies and Percentages of Influences and Barriers for Males in CT Programs for Survey Questions 41-60

Influences and Barriers[a]			
	Males in CT (n=39)		
	Not Applicable	Negative[b]	Neutral[c]	Positive[d]
Q41 Influenced by mother	3 (7.7%)	2 (5.1%)	5 (12.8%)	29 (74.4%)
Q42 Influenced by father	5 (12.8%)	3 (7.7%)	8 (20.5%)	23 (59.0%)
Q43 Influenced by sister	18 (46.2%)	2 (5.1%)	9 (23.1%)	10 (25.6%)

Q44 Influenced by brother	14 (35.9%)	4 (10.3%)	11 (28.2%)	10 (25.6%)
Q45 Influenced by children	24 (61.5%)	1 (2.6%)	5 (12.8%)	9 (23.1%)
Q46 Influenced by spouse	21 (53.8%)	2 (5.1%)	5 (12.8%)	11 (28.2%)
Q47 Influenced by other family members	6 (15.4%)	2 (5.1%)	12 (30.8%)	19 (48.7%)
Q48 Influenced by friends	7 (18.0%)	1 (2.6%)	9 (23.1%)	22 (56.4%)
Q49 Influenced by elementary school teachers	10 (25.6%)	6 (15.4%)	16 (41.0%)	7 (18.0%)
Q50 Influenced by middle school technology teachers	11 (28.2%)	4 (10.3%)	10 (25.6%)	14 (35.9%)
Q51 Influenced by high school technology teachers	10 (25.6%)	2 (5.1%)	11 (28.2%)	16 (41.0%)
Q52 Influenced by other teachers	11 (28.2%)	2 (5.1%)	14 (35.9%)	12 (30.8%)
Q53 Influenced by guidance counselors	11 (28.2%)	2 (5.1%)	10 (25.6%)	16 (41.0%)
Q54 Influenced by female high school classmates	10 (25.6%)	2 (5.1%)	12 (30.8%)	15 (38.5%)
Q55 Influenced by male high school classmates	10 (25.6%)	4 (10.3%)	14 (35.9%)	11 (28.2%)
Q56 Influenced by supervisors at work	17 (43.6%)	3 (7.7%)	11 (28.2%)	8 (20.5%)
Q57 Influenced by co-workers	18 (46.2%)	2 (5.1%)	7 (18.0%)	12 (30.8%)
Q58 Influenced by public figures	4 (10.3%)	2 (5.1%)	4 (10.3%)	29 (74.4%)
Q59 Influenced by fictional characters	6 (15.4%)	0 (0.0%)	10 (25.6%)	23 (59.0%)
Q60 Influenced by others	0 (0.0%)	0 (0.0%)	0 (0.0%)	39 (100%)

[a]Rounding errors may have prevented percentages from equaling 100%.
[b]Using 1-2 of Likert Scale.
[c]Using 3 of Likert Scale.
[d]Using 4-5 of Likert Scale.

A comparison of questions 41-60 for CT females and males revealed that the females were positively influenced more by brothers, sisters, children, and spouses more than males. Males were positively influenced more by parents, classmates, public figures, and fictional characters. All 39 (100%) listed that they were positively influenced by others and 12 of the 39 listed a comment in the comment section. Some of the responses were math teacher, mother-in-law, grandma, Jesus Christ, and stepdad. A higher percentage of the females than males were influenced by guidance counselors,

supervisors, and co-workers.

The data related to survey questions 41 - 60 for females and males in NT

programs are shown in Table 24 and 25.

Table 24

Frequencies and Percentages of Influences and Barriers Profiles for Females in NT
Programs for Survey Questions 41-60

Influences and Barriers[a]				
	Females in NT (n=91)			
	Not Applicable	Negative[b]	Neutral[c]	Positive[d]
Q41 Influenced by mother	7 (7.7%)	6 (6.6%)	15 (16.5%)	63 (69.2%)
Q42 Influenced by father	16 (17.6%)	12 (13.2%)	18 (19.8%)	45 (49.5%)
Q43 Influenced by sister	22 (24.2%)	8 (8.8%)	23 (25.3%)	38 (41.8%)
Q44 Influenced by brother	24 (26.4%)	7 (7.7%)	32 (35.2%)	28 (30.8%)
Q45 Influenced by children	74 (81.3%)	1 (1.1%)	5 (5.5%)	11 (12.1%)
Q46 Influenced by spouse	53 (58.2%)	4 (4.4%)	6 (6.6%)	28 (30.8%)
Q47 Influenced by other family members	4 (4.4%)	8 (8.8%)	21 (23.1%)	58 (63.7%)
Q48 Influenced by friends	4 (4.4%)	4 (4.4%)	30 (33.0%)	53 (58.2%)
Q49 Influenced by elementary school teachers	28 (30.8%)	3 (3.3%)	23 (25.3%)	37 (40.7%)
Q50 Influenced by middle school technology teachers	19 (20.9%)	8 (8.8%)	31 (34.1%)	33 (36.3%)
Q51 Influenced by high school technology teachers	15 (16.5%)	8 (8.8%)	19 (20.9%)	49 (53.8%)
Q52 Influenced by other teachers	15 (16.5%)	5 (5.5%)	31 (34.1%)	40 (44.0%)
Q53 Influenced by guidance counselors	18 (19.8%)	8 (8.8%)	21 (23.1%)	44 (48.4%)
Q54 Influenced by female high school classmates	10 (11.0%)	4 (4.4%)	33 (36.3%)	44 (48.4%)
Q55 Influenced by male high school classmates	17 (18.7%)	14 (15.4%)	31 (34.1%)	29 (31.9%)
Q56 Influenced by supervisors at work	27 (29.7%)	8 (8.8%)	20 (22.0%)	36 (39.6%)
Q57 Influenced by co-workers	25 (27.5%)	5 (5.5%)	29 (31.9%)	32 (35.2%)
Q58 Influenced by public	29 (31.9%)	4 (4.4%)	34 (37.4%)	24 (26.4%)

figures				
Q59 Influenced by fictional characters	30 (33.0%)	7 (7.7%)	34 (37.4%)	20 (22.0%)
Q60 Influenced by others	32 (35.2%)	2 (2.2%)	28 (30.8%)	29 (31.9%)

[a]Rounding errors may have prevented percentages from equaling 100%.
[b]Using 1-2 of Likert Scale.
[c]Using 3 of Likert Scale.
[d]Using 4-5 of Likert Scale.

Table 25

Frequencies and Percentages of Influences and Barriers for Males in NT Programs for Survey Questions 41-60

Influences and Barriers[a]			
Males in NT Programs (n=160)			
	Not Applicable	Negative[b]	Neutral[c]	Positive[d]
Q41 Influenced by mother	12 (7.5%)	17 (10.6%)	35 (21.9%)	96 (60.0%)
Q42 Influenced by father	20 (12.5%)	11 (6.9%)	31 (19.4%)	98 (61.3%)
Q43 Influenced by sister	63 (39.4%)	8 (5.0%)	40 (25.0%)	49 (30.6%)
Q44 Influenced by brother	43 (26.9%)	9 (5.6%)	43 (26.9%)	65 (40.6%)
Q45 Influenced by children	119 (74.4%)	2 (1.3%)	17 (10.6%)	22 (13.8%)
Q46 Influenced by spouse	102 (63.8%)	7 (4.4%)	10 (6.3%)	41 (25.6%)
Q47 Influenced by other family members	15 (9.4%)	12 (7.5%)	41 (25.6%)	92 (57.5%)
Q48 Influenced by friends	10 (6.3%)	10 (6.3%)	33 (20.6%)	107 (66.9%)
Q49 Influenced by elementary school teachers	46 (28.8%0	10 (6.3%)	46 (28.8%)	58 (36.3%)
Q50 Influenced by middle school technology teachers	52 (32.5%)	10 (6.3%)	43 (26.9%)	55 (34.4%)
Q51 Influenced by high school technology teachers	32 (20.0%)	10 (6.3%)	32 (20.0%)	86 (53.8%)
Q52 Influenced by other teachers	42 (26.3%)	8 (5.0%)	34 (21.3%)	76 (47.5%)
Q53 Influenced by guidance counselors	31 (19.4%)	10 (6.3%)	40 (25.0%)	79 (49.4%)
Q54 Influenced by female high school classmates	28 (17.4%)	15 (9.4%)	48 (30.0%)	69 (43.1%)
Q55 Influenced by male high school classmates	22 (13.8%)	25 (15.6%)	52 (32.5%)	61 (38.1%)
Q56 Influenced by supervisors at work	48 (30.0%)	11 (6.9%)	45 (28.1%)	56 (35.0%)
Q57 Influenced by co-workers	52 (32.5%)	11 (6.9%)	43 (26.9%)	54 (33.8%)

Q58 Influenced by public figures	45 (28.1%)	14 (8.8%)	57 (35.6%)	44 (27.5%)
Q59 Influenced by fictional characters	59 (36.9%)	8 (5.0%)	61 (38.1%)	32 (20.0%)
Q60 Influenced by others	56 (35.0%)	5 (3.1%)	45 (28.1%)	54 (33.8%)

[a]Rounding errors may have prevented percentages from equaling 100%.
[b]Using 1-2 of Likert Scale.
[c]Using 3 of Likert Scale.
[d]Using 4-5 of Likert Scale.

A comparison of questions 41-60 for females and males in NT programs revealed that a higher percentage of NT females than NT males were positively influenced by their mothers, but a higher percentage of NT males were positively influenced more by their fathers than NT females.

More NT females were influenced by sisters, spouses, other members of the family, and friends than NT males. Males and females were almost equally influenced by teachers and career counselors. More NT females were influenced by female classmates than NT males and more NT males were influenced by male classmates than NT female students. A considerable higher percentage of the NT male students were influenced by supervisors, co-workers, public figures, and fictional characters than NT females, but these percentages were still relatively low.

Summary of Influences and Barriers Profiles Comparing Male and Female Students in CT and NT Programs

The CT and NT groups were grouped by gender in answer to the fourth research question. The use of computers in school and at home during school years was similar for all four groups, but not significantly influential in the career decision-making process. They all used computers less in elementary school than in later school years. Females in CT used technology slightly less during their school years than the other three groups, but

149

since they were older, it is consistent with the other three groups. However, males in both CT (79.5%) and NT (75.6%) had a higher percentage than CT (61.9%) and NT (64.8%) females of currently owning a computer. The CT males (53.8%) currently play computer games substantially more than CT females (11.9%) while NT males (39.4%) and females (44.0%) were somewhat the same and less than CT males, but considerably more than CT females. Opportunities to *use* and *learn* new technologies had larger percentages for both male and female CT students than male and female NT students.

Negative images, derogatory comments, and gender discrimination did not have any substantial influence with any of the four groups and was somewhat similar for each group. Perceived working conditions in a technology field were considerably higher for CT females (46.3%) and males (64.1%) than for NT females (17.6%) or males (13.1%), so it may have been an influence instead of a barrier. Student perception about productive by using technology and simplifying data collection was similar for all four groups with the CT students reporting a slightly higher percentage than the NT students, but all four groups agreeing that technology improved student productive and data collection. Students in CT programs were more comfortable with computers than the students in the NT programs, but all were very comfortable with computers.

Family members were a positive influence for the most part with only three categories reporting a negative influence above 10%: Male CT brothers (10.3%); female NT fathers (13.2%); and male NT mothers (10.6%). Friends were notably positive in all four groups. School teachers were positive with no real significance, except that technology teachers were the most positive of elementary, middle school, and other high school teachers for all four groups in the study. Counselors, classmates, co-workers, and supervisors either reported positive influence, neutral, or not applicable, with very small percentages reporting a negative influence. Computer technology males reported significantly higher percentages of positive influence from public figures and fictional characters than the other three groups.

Opportunities to use and learn new technologies, perceived working conditions in technology, and personal contacts contribute positive influences to career decisions. There was no evidence that derogatory comments about technology, negative images of technologists, or gender discrimination were barriers in the career decision-making process.

Research Question Five

How does the model identified in this study for choosing a computer technology career compare to existing career choice models?

Existing Career Choice Models

Logical comparison of existing career models to a new model emerging from this study has been used to answer research question number five. There are many types of career models that focus on interests, abilities, and skills that are used by teachers, counselors, and individuals to determine what type of employment matches personality, education, and plans for the future.

"The context in which career decisions are commonly made is dynamic: occupations are changing rapidly, society is becoming increasingly complex and multicultural, and individuals need to plan for diverging rather than converging career paths" (Magnusson, 1995, ¶ 1). Career models are used to determine what educational route is needed to obtain goals (Gray & Herr, 1998). Existing models consist of development models, linear models, classic counseling models, contextual models and others. "A major criticism of prevailing theories is that they are based on male experiences" (Kerka, 1992, ¶ 4).

Formal decision-making models were used to confirm decisions instead of determine a suitable career choice (Magnusson, 1995). "The classic career counseling models have focused primarily on practical and prescriptive methods" (Miller-Tiedeman, 1999, p. 1), but the new models do not just focus on just the job. The current new models deal with the theory of life, "focusing on logical, emotional, and spiritual facets of one's life" (p. 2).

The Self-Determined Career Development Model (SDCDM) was developed to support adult job and career outcomes, primarily for students in vocational rehabilitation "to enable persons with disabilities to obtain the careers and jobs they want" (wnyilp.org, 2006, p. 3). The instructional portion of the model requires the students "to develop and use self-directed goal setting and problem solving skills to set educational goals" (p. 4). The model's three-phase process allows teachers to support students to learn self-direction skills and goal attainment. It helps the students identify the problem, potential solutions, barriers, and consequences.

Model Identified in this Study: Moody's Model

This study takes a more focused approach to career decisions in technology. The influences and barriers identified in this study have contributed to the development of a new model designed specifically to describe factors that may impact the decisions of male and female students to choose a career in computing technology. This new Moody's Model focus on career decision-making in computer technology at career technology level, and is based on identifying gender-specific barriers and influences that can impact this particular career choices. Moody's Model, discussed and shown graphically in Chapter five, presents some important patterns not identified in previous career choice models and research literature. These include:

1. Lack of parental employment in a technology field as a technology career decision influence.

2. Lack of specific program assistance and career counseling at the CarerTech level.

3. Lack of evidence playing with computer games as a child or currently.

4. Ability to use/learn new technologies was more influential in contributing to the technology career selection than past or present technology usage.

5. Lack of influence of negative perception about technology and computing careers.

6. Positive perceptions about technology and computing careers contributed to selection of computer technology careers.

7. Lack of evidence of derogatory comments as a barrier to choosing a computer career.

8. Lack of evidence of gender discrimination as a barrier to choosing a computer career.

9. Importance of influence of family in career decisions.

10. Importance of influence of friends in career decisions.

11. Importance of high school technology teachers in career decisions.

These findings and their synthesis in Moody's Model suggest collectively that in the specific case of career decisions at CareerTech level regarding careers in computer technology, some new dynamics may be at work. As times and technology change, so may career decision dynamics. These possibilities are explained in Chapter Five.

CHAPTER V

SUMMARY, RECOMMENDATIONS, AND CONCLUSIONS

Summary

In a perfect society, there would be no queen bees, drones, or workers. Everyone would be equal. But work has to be done and the hive functions smoother when work is divided into specialized areas, so it operates as a community. People have grouped together to form communities to maximize productivity, conveniences, employment, and inventions. Society has created specialized jobs to improve human life style, but not everyone can be the president, a football player, or jet fighter. Career decisions are not limited to birth rights as a queen bee, but are affected by many internal and external factors. Influences and barriers on career decisions begin at birth and knowledge about those influences and barriers may help facilitate career making decisions.

The purpose of this study was to examine influences and barriers that affect career decisions for computer technology students and non-technology students and related gender differentiation to develop a gender-specific career choice model impacting selection of computer technology careers at CareerTech level. The general goal was to gain more understanding of the decision making process and create a building block for more research and understanding of female recruitment in technology fields. Specific goals of this study were to depict existing conditions, explain gathered data from student responses with numerical indices and graphic forms, and gain more understanding of the decision making process of selecting a major in a computer technology field using descriptive statistics. An online questionnaire was used to collect demographic data and technological information about influences and barriers for career decision-making.

The sample (N=424) for this study were current students that were 18 or older and attending a Technology Center in the Oklahoma CareerTech system. Frequencies and percentages from the responses to 60 survey questions were used to compare data from computer technology and non-technology students and male and female students to identify career decision influences and barriers. There were more NT students (251) than CT students (173). There were more NT male students (160) than CT female students (134), NT female students (91), or CT male students (n=39).

Conclusions: Demographical Profiles

The demographics data revealed that the participants of this study attended the campuses located in towns or rural areas instead of the metro campuses and that the participants lived in towns or rural areas. The majority of the students were Caucasian, young, single, and from lower social economic families. Majorities were also admitted into their first choice of programs, did not have to go through a selection process to be admitted, received very little career counseling while attending the CareerTech, and did not have parents working in a technology field.

There were few minorities that participated in this study, which might be a result of DuBois' views about vocational education restricting promotion of blacks in America. DuBois' views have influenced decisions about whether African Americans should attend CareerTech schools or not. Contrary to Booker T. Washington's beliefs that the way out of poverty and slavery was to develop a trade, DuBois emphatically believed that the promotion of vocational education limited African Americans. Many African American parents refused to let their children attend vocational programs (Gibson, 1978; Washington, 2001). The majority of the students in this study were Caucasian, however Native Americans had higher percentages than other ethnic groups and higher percentages for students in the CT programs than the NT programs. There were limited numbers of minorities in any of the groups, especially Asian.

Most parents did not work in a computer technology field, however there were more mothers than fathers working in technology which contradicts research literature. Also, males reported more parents working in the technology fields than females.

Females were more evenly spread across age groups and had greater age range, especially the CT females. Computer technology females were older in nature, fewer who were single, more who were post-secondary, fewer with siblings at home, more assistance with career counseling, and more in the lower social-economic income levels. The CT students had a higher percentage who reported disabilities and disadvantages. Both groups of females reported having to go through a selection process to be admitted into the program of choice more than males. Both groups of males were younger, still in high school, and in higher income brackets. The CT males were more likely to be admitted into their first choice of CareerTech programs.

Conclusions: Career Decision Influences and Barriers

Previous usage of technology in school and at home does not appear to positively influence decisions when selecting CT careers, but opportunities to use and learn new technologies does appear to influence career decisions. Lack of these opportunities may be barriers to choosing a CT career.

All groups were positively influence by family and friends. The CT males were influenced by fictional characters and public figures. The Crown Financial Ministries (2006) published advice for parents reporting that even with the influence of media, friends, Internet, and teachers, "parents are still the primary influence that affects their children's career decisions" (¶ 6).

Contrary to literature review the negative images of technology people and jobs was not a factor. Verbick (2001) reported "women face sexism from their male peers, have a lack of role models in the industry, and are socially conditioned to think that computers are for men only" (241). Also derogatory statements or negative comments did not have an influence in avoiding or selecting technology education in this study. There did not appear to be issues of gender discrimination as indicated in current research.

There are counseling programs available at CareerTech facilities, but few students qualify or take advantage of the opportunities. However, more females reported using the available counseling resources than males. High school counselors and high school technology teachers were reported as highly positive and influential in selecting a career.

Computer technology was better represented by females than males in this study. The females were older and had opportunities to use and learn technology which may be instrumental in their career choices. There were fewer females in other non-traditional careers such as auto, construction, and etc., but more males were enrolled in NT such as auto mechanics, carpentry, and etc. The NT groups were less comfortable, supportive, positive, and impressed with computers which are factors for not selecting technology careers.

Moody's Model

Existing career choice models began in conjunction with vocational education

(Gray & Herr, 1998) and used interest, skills, and training to help suggest career choices

(Verbick, 2002) Emerging technology and expanded of technology has changed many

careers resulting in different methods for choosing a career.

Literature has addressed issues of gender discrimination (Hawkes &

Brockmueller, 2004; Reskin & Hartmann, 1986; Sanders & Nelson, 2004), stereotyping,

negative perceptions of a technologist/computer scientist (Brock, 2002), lack of role

models (Boitel, 2002; Verbick, 2002), inappropriate counseling (Read, 2002), and other

influences and barriers that have impacted females in selecting technology careers. This

study found more females than males in computer technology programs, but the National

percentages of females in computer technology professions is still substantially less than

males working in a technology field (National, 2006). Those influences and barriers have

been used to develop a career model specific to counseling CareerTech students making

career-decisions.

Moody's Model is a new model incorporating the findings of this study, designed

to assist students interested in attending a CareerTech program better understand the

influences and barriers surrounding computer technology careers. The model should be

helpful in recruiting females into technology and counseling all students about the

influences and barriers of technology careers.

MOODY'S MODEL

Gender-Specific Influences and Barriers Impacting Selection of Computer Technology Careers at CareerTech

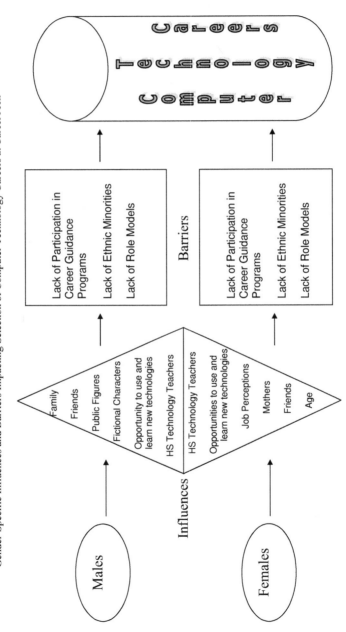

Recommendations for Practice

There was no evidence of gender discrimination, rejection of technology careers because of negative perceptions, or influence from derogatory comments about technology professions. So, it may be time to move past those perceived issues and concentrate on more prevalent issues and stop talking about gender bias.

More career counseling using factors in new career models to help guide students into computing careers is a recommendation from this study. The barriers and influences identified in this study can be used for guidance purposes. Since high school teachers, especially technology teachers, and career counselors present positive influences, they might represent role models for a beginning to improve career guidance.

Opportunities to use and learn new technologies was an indicator of technology career selection and providing such say opportunities is a recommendation for recruiting both female and male students at all levels of schooling. Since public figures and fictional characters were an influence for male computer technology students, who were younger in nature, special programs to promote technology careers might use role models, public figures, or fictional characters as a spokesperson. Families and friends were identified as a positive influence, and could be instrumental in promoting technology careers.

Recommendations for Further Research

As technology careers expand and change, career decision-making models will change, especially computer technology career models. Continued research is needed to understand the influences and barriers associated with career decision-making for computer technology, but not limited to computer technology. Because of the influence in most professions due to the continued expansion of technology in many areas, career choices will be altered. Recommendations for further research from this study specifically for computer technology are:

1. More research in regards to the influence of friends and if positive influence is supportive agreement or influential in decision-making.

2. More research concerning siblings, specifically idolization of older siblings.

3. Qualitative research to determine perceived images of computer technologist.

4. Qualitative research with reference to gender discrimination.

5. Qualitative research about selection processes for different computer technology programs.

6. Specific studies to determine why CareerTech males enroll in other programs instead of computer technology programs.

7. Specific studies to determine why computer technology males attending a four year college did not attend a computer technology program at an Oklahoma CareerTech Center?

8. Compare influences and barriers of CareerTech computer technology students to four year university computer technology students.

9. CareerTech Programs have reorganized the career cluster model and placed an emphasis on clusters in curriculum and teaching. Students will have a broader range of related occupations. This suggests potential for further research in career decision making areas.

10. Some counseling programs, such as TANF at post-secondary level, require entry to higher-tech, high-wage programs. What influence might this have in computer technology career choices? Did post-secondary students choose computer

technology because they wanted it or because they could get funding in high-tech programs?

11. Further studies to determine why females are choosing computer technology careers.

12. Further studies to determine how high school counselors advise females concerning computer technology career choices.

13. What other factors not included in this study may have influenced career decisions?

14. Further research to determine the ethnic distribution in industry, of CareerTech teachers, and CareerTech students. Why is there under representation of minorities in technical careers at the sub-baccalaureate level?

15. Evaluate opportunities to learn about and use technology/computers. How much impact does opportunity influence computer technology career choices?

16. Have programs for young students had an impact on career choices?

Conclusion

It appears that older female non-traditional students have opportunities at work, home, or school to use and learn new technologies and that has influenced them to pursue technology careers through the CareerTech Centers. There might be a paradigm shift in the technology fields as more females make career decisions to enter technology fields at the CareerTech level. This study and the development of Moody's Model were designed to assist in promotion of those changes. As the fear of technology dissolves and new technology career models are used, there may be a greater chance of encouraging females to enter technology careers.

REFERENCES

Barker, T. (1998). *Technology education must welcome females.* Viewed on January 10, 2005 at http://www.bsu.edu/news/article/0,1370,-1019-628,00.html.

Brown, B. (2003). Career Education Modles. ERIC Clearinghouse on Adult, Career, and Vocational Education, Center on Education and training or Employment. The Ohio State University. (ERIC Document Reproduction Service No. ED 44).

Carnevale, A. P., Gainer, L. J., & Meltzer, A. S. (1990). *Workplace basics: The essential skills employers want.* San Francisco, CA: Jossey-Bass. Retrieved on October 20, 2003, from http://www.ncwd-youth.info/assets/research_briefs/ Preparatory%20 Experiences _HSHT_research%20brief.pdf.

Cavanagh, S. (2002). Advocates Call for Breakdown of Gender Barriers in Vocational Education. *Education Week.* Viewed on January 4, 2005 at http://www.edweek.org/ew/newstory.cfm?slug=40voced.h21.

Clark, D. (2001). Learning domains or Bloom's taxonomy. Retrieved November 1, 2005 from http://www.nwlink.com/~donclark/hrd/bloom.html.

Computer Schools (2004). *Women in the IT Industry.* Viewed on March 4, 2004 at http://Computer-schools.us/Women-in-the-IT-Industry.htm.

Edwards, R., Ranson, S., & Strain, M. (2002). *Reflexivity: towards a theory of lifelong learning.* International Journal of Lifelong Education, VOL. 21, No. 6 (November-December 2002), 525-536.

Eisenberg, B. and Ruthsdotter, M. (1998). Living the Legacy: The Women's Rights Movement. 1848 – 1998 (2002). *The National Women's History Project.* Viewed on December 10, 2004 at http://www.legacy98.org/move-hist.html.

Elias, J. and Merriam, S. (1998). Philosophical Foundations of Adult Education, 2nd Ed.

Equal Rights Advocates (June, 2003). *Sex Discrimination.* Viewed on December 10, 2004 at http://www.equalrights.org/sexdiscrim/info.htm.

Fischer, G. (1996). *Making learning a part of life beyond the "gift wrapping" approach to technology.* University of Colorado, Boulder. Available online: http://cs.colorado.edu/~13d/philosophy.html.

164

Fogg, P. (2005). Harvard's President Wonders Aloud About Women in Science and Math. *The Chronicle of Higher Education.* Volume LI, number 21. p. A12.

Gibson, R. (1978). Booker T. Washington and W.E.B. Debois: The problem of Negro leadership. Yale-New Haven Teachers Institute. Viewed on November 2, 2006 at http://www.yale.edu/ynhti/curriculum/units/1978/2/78.02.02.x.html.

Gray, K. and Herr, E. (1998). *Workforce Education, the Basics.* Needham Heights, MA: Allan and Bacon.

Gurian, M. and Stevens, K. (2004). With Boys and Girls in Mind, *Educational Leadership.* Vol. 62, 3. p. 6-15.

Harvard (2006). Viewed on November 3, 2006 at http://www-tech.mit.edu/V125/N2/long3_2.2w.html.

Hayes, C. D. *(1998).* Quoted in *How about: life, liberty, and the pursuit of wisdom?* Retrieved September 13, 2003, from http://www.bookflash.com/releases/100055.html.

Hemel, D. (2005). Published on Monday, January 17, 2005. *Summers' Comments on Women and Science* Draw Ire Crimson Staff Writer. Viewed on February 13, 2005 at http://www.thecrimson.com/article.aspx?ref=505349.

Henderson, R and Robertson, M. (1999). Who wants to be an entrepreneur? Young adult attitudes to entrepreneurship as a career. Research paper. MCB UP Ltd. Vol. 41, 5 p. 241.

Herring, S. (1999).The Rhetorical Dynamics of Gender Harassment On-Line. *The Information Society.* Vol. 15. pp. 151-167.

Hoye, J. D. & Drier, H. (1999). Career education: The foundation for school-to-work. In A. J. Paulter, Jr. (Ed.), *Workforce education: Issues for the new century.* (pp. 65-73). Prakken Publications, Inc.: Ann Arbor, MI.

Intel (2004). Women online have new tech attitude, according to survey: Survey reveals new woman emerging. M2Presswire. *Coventry*: December 9, 2004. Viewed on January 25, 2005 at http://proquest.umi.com/pqdweb?index.

Isi.salford.ac.uk (2006) Women in Information Technology. Retrieved on April 2, 2006 at www. Isi.salford.ac.uk/gris/winit/index.html.

NSF News (2004). *NSF Funds $3.25M Award To Boost Women's Involvement in IT.* Viewed on November 11, 2004 at http://www.tgc.com/hpcwireWWW/04/1022/108633.html.

National Education Goals Panel, (1995). *The national education goals report: Building a nation of learners 1995.* Washington, D.C.

National Women's Law Center (2000). Title IX. A report of the National Coalition for Women and Girls in Education.

National Women's Law Center (2002). *Title IX at 30 Report Card on Gender Equity.* A Report of the National Coalition for Women and Girls in Education.

Oklahoma Department of Career and Technology Education. (n.d.). *Careertech key message.* Retrieved October 22, 2003, from http://www.okcareertech.org/pio/features /keymessage.htm.

Overtoom, C. (2000). *Employability skills: An update.* ERIC Digest No. 220. Columbus ERIC clearing House on Adult, Career and Vocational Education, The Ohio State University. (EDO-EC-00-220).

Pucel, D. J. (1999). Curriculum issues. In A. J. Paulter, Jr. (Ed.), *Workforce education: Issues for the new century.* (pp. 211-222). Prakken Publications, Inc.: Ann Arbor, MI.

Peck, B. T. (1996). *European lifelong leaning initiatives.* Phi Delta Kappan, 77(9), 645.

Quinley J.W. & Hickman R.C. (2002). *Work place the need for workforce development: What research tells us.* Retrieved October 12, 2003, from http://www.ncwe.org/ workplace/needworkforcedevelopment.htm.

Read, B. (2002). Unlocking the Clubhouse: Women in Computing, 2 Professors Offer Advice on Making Computer Science More Open to Women, *The Chronicle of Higher Education*, Information Technology. Volume LI, number 19.

Reskin, B. and Hartmann, H. (1986). Women's Work, Men's Work: Sex Segregation on the Job. National Academies Press.

Roomb7 (2004). *Women in Technology: Non-Traditional Careers for Women.* Viewed on March 4, 2004 at http://wwww.roomb7.com.

Sanders, J. and Nelson, S. (2004) Closing Gender Gaps in Science. *Educational Leadership.* Vol. 21, pp. 74-77.

Secretary's Commission on Achieving Necessary Skills. (1991). *What work requires of schools: A SCANS report for America 2000.* Washington, D.C.: U.S. Department of Labor.

Secretary's Commission on Achieving Necessary Skills. (1992). *Learning a living: A blueprint for high performance: A SCANS report for America 2000.* Washington, D. C.: U.S. Department of Labor.

Sears, S. J. & Hersh, S. B. (1998). Contextual teaching and learning: An overview of the project. Contextual teaching and learning; Preparing teachers to enhance student success in and beyond school. The Ohio State University College of Education in partnership with Bowling Green State University.

Strauss, M. J., Shaffer, S., Kaser J., and Shaw, K. (1991). *Gender Bias in Mathematics, Science and Technology: The Report Card # 3.* Computer Science's Gender Gap.

Summers, L. (2005) *Remarks at NBER Conference on Diversifying the Science & Engineering Workforce.* Viewed on March 29, 2005 at http://www.president.harvard.edu/speeches/2005/nber.html.

TechPrep (2004). *Women in Technology.* Viewed on March 4, 2004 at http://www.bristolcommunitycollege.edu/techprep/wit.html.

Verbick, T. (2002). *Women, Technology, and Gender Bias.* Owens Library 122B, Northwest Missouri State University. Maryville, Missouri.

Washington, E. (2001). DuBois vs. Washington: Old lessons black people have not learned. Issues & Views. Viewed on November 2, 2006 at http://www.issues-views.com/index.php/sect/1000/article/999.

Wakefield, J. (2002). *Tempting women into tech jobs.* Viewed on January 17, 2004 at http:/news.bbc.co.uk/1/hi/technology/1761669.stm.

Wakefield, J. (2003). *Women spurning tech jobs.* Viewed on January 17, 2004 at http:/news.bbc.co.uk/1/hi/technology/2687247.stm.

Wickwire, P. (2001). A perspective on career education in the USA AACE distinguished member series on career education. Paper presented at the world congress Commemoration of the 50th Anniversary of the International Association for Educational and Vocational Guidance, Paris, France, September 20 (ED 465863).

Woodard, C.A. (May, 2005). Career shock: A study of late baby boomers pursuing career change through formal learning.

APPENDICES

APPENDIX A

Survey Questionnaire

Career Decisions

Part I Demographics

Please select the appropriate response for each of the following questions.

1) What is your gender?

☐ Female

☐ Male

2) What is your age?

☐

3) What is your race?

☐ Caucasian/White

☐ African American

☐ Native American or Indigenous

☐ Asian/Pacific Islander

☐ Hispanic

☐ Latino

☐ Multiracial

☐ Other (please specify)

If you selected other, please specify:

170

4) What is your grade classification?

☐ Junior

☐ Senior

☐ Post-secondary

☐ Other (please specify)

If you selected other, please specify:

5) Are you receiving any special career counseling services?

☐ Dropout Recovery

☐ TANF

☐ Displaced Homemaker

☐ None

☐ Other (please specify)

If you selected other, please specify:

6) What is the name of the CareerTech program in which you are currently enrolled?

7) Was this your first choice?

☐ Yes

☐ No (Specify in comment box)

Additional comments:

8) Was there a selection process for either program?

☐ Yes (Specify in comment box)
☐ No

Additional comments:

9) Where do you reside?

☐ Urban (Oklahoma City or Tulsa)
☐ Suburban (residential region near a major city)
☐ Town
☐ Rural

10) What is your household income?

☐ Under $9,999
☐ $10,000-$19,999
☐ $20,000-$29,999
☐ $30,000-$39,999
☐ $40,000-$49,999
☐ $50,000-$59,999
☐ $60,000-$69,999
☐ $70,000-$79,999
☐ $80,000-$89,999
☐ Over $90,000

11) What is your marital status?

☐ Divorced
☐ Married
☐ Separated
☐ Single
☐ Widowed

12) How many children under the age of 18 live in your household?

☐ None
☐ 1
☐ 2
☐ 3
☐ 4 or more

13) Does your father work in a computer technology field?

☐ Yes
☐ No
☐ Not Sure

14) Does your mother work in a computer technology field?

☐ Yes
☐ No
☐ Not Sure

15) Do you have a disability? (Select all that apply.)

☐ Vision impaired (Non-correctable)
☐ Hearing impaired
☐ Impaired motor development
☐ Cognitively disadvantaged
☐ Academically disadvantaged
☐ Economically disadvantaged
☐ Not impaired or disadvantaged

16) Which Career Tech campus do you attend?

☐ Autry

☐ Caddo-Kiowa

☐ Canadian Valley - Chickasha

☐ Canadian Valley - El Reno

☐ Central Tech - Sapulpa

☐ Central Tech - Drumright

☐ Chisholm Trail

☐ Eastern Oklahoma County

☐ Francis Tuttle - Portland

☐ Francis Tuttle - Rockwell

☐ Gordon Cooper

☐ Great Plains - Tillman-Kiowa

☐ Great Plains - Lawton

☐ Green Country

☐ High Plains

☐ Indian Capital - Bill Willis

☐ Indian Capital - Muskogee

☐ Indian Capital Sallisaw

☐ Indian Capital - Stilwell

☐ Kiamichi - Atoka

☐ Kiamichi - Durant

☐ Kiamichi - Hugo

☐ Kiamichi - Idabel

☐ Kiamichi - McAlester

☐ Kiamichi - Poteau

☐ Kiamichi - Spiro

☐ Kiamichi - Stigler

☐ Kiamichi - Talihina

☐ Meridian

☐ Metro Tech - Adult & Cont. Education

174

- ☐ Metro Tech - Aviation Career Center
- ☐ Metro Tech - South Bryant
- ☐ Metro Tech - Springlake
- ☐ Mid-America
- ☐ Mid-Del
- ☐ Moore Norman
- ☐ Northeast - East Campus
- ☐ Northeast - North Campus
- ☐ Northeast - South Campus
- ☐ Northwest - Alva
- ☐ Northwest - Fairview
- ☐ Pioneer
- ☐ Pontotoc
- ☐ Red River
- ☐ Southern Oklahoma
- ☐ Southwest
- ☐ Tri County
- ☐ Tulsa Tech - Broken Arrow
- ☐ Tulsa Tech - Lemley
- ☐ Tulsa Tech - Peoria
- ☐ Tulsa Tech - Riverside
- ☐ Wes Watkins
- ☐ Western - Burns Flat
- ☐ Western - Sayre
- ☐ Western - Weatherford

Next Page (1 of 3)

Part II

Technological History

Please indicate your level of exposure or experience to each of the following statements.

---

17) I used computers at elementary school.

☐ Very Often

☐ Often

☐ Sometimes

☐ Rarely

☐ Never

18) I used computers at middle school.

☐ Very Often

☐ Often

☐ Sometimes

☐ Rarely

☐ Never

19) I used computers at high school.

☐ Very Often

☐ Often

☐ Sometimes

☐ Rarely

☐ Never

20) I used computers at home during elementary school.

☐ Very Often

☐ Often

☐ Sometimes

☐ Rarely

☐ Never

21) I used computers at home during middle school.

☐ Very Often
☐ Often
☐ Sometimes
☐ Rarely
☐ Never

22) I used computers at home during high school.

☐ Very Often
☐ Often
☐ Sometimes
☐ Rarely
☐ Never

23) I currently have a computer at home.

☐ Very Often
☐ Often
☐ Sometimes
☐ Rarely
☐ Never

24) I currently use a cell phone.

☐ Very Often
☐ Often
☐ Sometimes
☐ Rarely
☐ Never

25) I played computer games (Nintendo, Play Station, & Etc.) as a child.

☐ Very Often
☐ Often
☐ Sometimes
☐ Rarely
☐ Never

26) I currently play computer games (Nintendo, Play Station, & Etc.).

☐ Very Often
☐ Often
☐ Sometimes
☐ Rarely
☐ Never

27) I have opportunities to use new technologies.

☐ Very Often
☐ Often
☐ Sometimes
☐ Rarely
☐ Never

28) I have opportunities to learn new technologies.

☐ Very Often
☐ Often
☐ Sometimes
☐ Rarely
☐ Never

Please indicate your level of agreement or disagreement with each of the following statements.

---

29) I believe negative images about computer scientists influenced my career decisions.

☐ Strongly Agree

☐ Agree

☐ Neutral

☐ Disagree

☐ Strongly Disagree

30) I believe perceived working conditions about computer jobs influenced my career decisions.

☐ Strongly Agree

☐ Agree

☐ Neutral

☐ Disagree

☐ Strongly Disagree

31) I believe derogatory comments about technology careers influenced my career decisions.

☐ Strongly Agree

☐ Agree

☐ Neutral

☐ Disagree

☐ Strongly Disagree

32) I believe I have been discriminated against because of my gender.

☐ Strongly Agree

☐ Agree

☐ Neutral

☐ Disagree

☐ Strongly Disagree

33) I believe computers and technology have made students more productive.

☐ Strongly Agree

☐ Agree

☐ Neutral

☐ Disagree

☐ Strongly Disagree

34) I believe technology takes the human element out of work and life.

☐ Strongly Agree

☐ Agree

☐ Neutral

☐ Disagree

☐ Strongly Disagree

35) I believe gathering data for class assignments is simplified by using computers.

☐ Strongly Agree

☐ Agree

☐ Neutral

☐ Disagree

☐ Strongly Disagree

36) I am comfortable when using computers for student assignments.

☐ Strongly Agree

☐ Agree

☐ Neutral

☐ Disagree

☐ Strongly Disagree

37) I prefer getting information from a printed page instead of a computer screen.

☐ Strongly Agree

☐ Agree

☐ Neutral

☐ Disagree

☐ Strongly Disagree

38) I believe the frustrations created by computers are more trouble than they are worth.

☐ Strongly Agree

☐ Agree

☐ Neutral

☐ Disagree

☐ Strongly Disagree

39) I believe schools spend too much money on computers.

☐ Strongly Agree

☐ Agree

☐ Neutral

☐ Disagree

☐ Strongly Disagree

40) I believe technology frees people from tedious work allowing them to concentrate on more rewarding tasks.

☐ Strongly Agree

☐ Agree

☐ Neutral

☐ Disagree

☐ Strongly Disagree

Part III **Influences and Barriers**

Select the degree of positive or negative influences that each of the following sources had on your career decisions. If a source is not relevant to you, select Not Applicable.

41) Mother

☐ Very Positive

☐ Somewhat Positive

☐ Neutral

☐ Somewhat Negative

☐ Very Negative

☐ Not Applicable

42) Father

☐ Very Positive

☐ Somewhat Positive

☐ Neutral

☐ Somewhat Negative

☐ Very Negative

☐ Not Applicable

43) Sister(s)

☐ Very Positive

☐ Somewhat Positive

☐ Neutral

☐ Somewhat Negative

☐ Very Negative

☐ Not Applicable

44) Brother(s)

☐ Very Positive
☐ Somewhat Positive
☐ Neutral
☐ Somewhat Negative
☐ Very Negative
☐ Not Applicable

45) Your children

☐ Very Positive
☐ Somewhat Positive
☐ Neutral
☐ Somewhat Negative
☐ Very Negative
☐ Not Applicable

46) Spouse or Significant other

☐ Very Positive
☐ Somewhat Positive
☐ Neutral
☐ Somewhat Negative
☐ Very Negative
☐ Not Applicable

47) Other family members

☐ Very Positive
☐ Somewhat Positive
☐ Neutral
☐ Somewhat Negative
☐ Very Negative
☐ Not Applicable

183

48) Friends

☐ Very Positive

☐ Somewhat Positive

☐ Neutral

☐ Somewhat Negative

☐ Very Negative

☐ Not Applicable

49) Elementary school teachers

☐ Very Positive

☐ Somewhat Positive

☐ Neutral

☐ Somewhat Negative

☐ Very Negative

☐ Not Applicable

50) Middle school technology teachers

☐ Very Positive

☐ Somewhat Positive

☐ Neutral

☐ Somewhat Negative

☐ Very Negative

☐ Not Applicable

51) High school technology teachers

☐ Very Positive

☐ Somewhat Positive

☐ Neutral

☐ Somewhat Negative

☐ Very Negative

☐ Not Applicable

52) Other middle and high school teachers

☐ Very Positive

☐ Somewhat Positive

☐ Neutral

☐ Somewhat Negative

☐ Very Negative

☐ Not Applicable

53) Guidance Counselors

☐ Very Positive

☐ Somewhat Positive

☐ Neutral

☐ Somewhat Negative

☐ Very Negative

☐ Not Applicable

54) Female high school classmates

☐ Very Positive

☐ Somewhat Positive

☐ Neutral

☐ Somewhat Negative

☐ Very Negative

☐ Not Applicable

55) Male high school classmates

☐ Very Positive

☐ Somewhat Positive

☐ Neutral

☐ Somewhat Negative

☐ Very Negative

☐ Not Applicable

56) Supervisor at work

☐ Very Positive

☐ Somewhat Positive

☐ Neutral

☐ Somewhat Negative

☐ Very Negative

☐ Not Applicable

57) Co-workers

☐ Very Positive

☐ Somewhat Positive

☐ Neutral

☐ Somewhat Negative

☐ Very Negative

☐ Not Applicable

58) Public figure (Real person in media, sports, politics, history, etc. Identify public figure in additional comments section.)

☐ Very Positive

☐ Somewhat Positive

☐ Neutral

☐ Somewhat Negative

☐ Very Negative

☐ Not Applicable

Additional comments:

59) Fictional character (Character in book, movie, television, etc. Identify fictional character in additional comments section.)

☐ Very Positive
☐ Somewhat Positive
☐ Neutral
☐ Somewhat Negative
☐ Very Negative
☐ Not Applicable

Additional comments:

60) Other person in your life (Identify other person in additional comments section.)

☐ Very Positive
☐ Somewhat Positive
☐ Neutral
☐ Somewhat Negative
☐ Very Negative
☐ Not Applicable

Additional comments:

Thank you for taking the time to complete this online questionnaire and participate in this research.

Submit Survey (3 of 3)

187

APPENDIX B

INSTITUTIONAL REVIEW BOARD APPROVAL

Oklahoma State University Institutional Review Board

Date: Monday, October 17, 2005

IRB Application No ED0642

Proposal Title: Choosing Careers in Computer Technology Fields: Influences, Barriers, and Gender in Computer Technology Fields

Reviewed and Exempt
Processed as:

Status Recommended by Reviewer(s): Approved   Protocol Expires: 10/16/2006

Principal
Investigator(s

Judy Moody   Lynna Ausburn
Box 911   217 Willard
Muskogee, OK 74402   Stillwater, OK 74078

The IRB application referenced above has been approved. It is the judgment of the reviewers that the rights and welfare of individuals who may be asked to participate in this study will be respected, and that the research will be conducted in a manner consistent with the IRB requirements as outlined in section 45 CFR 46.

✓ The final versions of any printed recruitment, consent and assent documents bearing the IRB approval stamp are attached to this letter. These are the versions that must be used during the study.

As Principal Investigator, it is your responsibility to do the following:

1. Conduct this study exactly as it has been approved. Any modifications to the research protocol must be submitted with the appropriate signatures for IRB approval.
2. Submit a request for continuation if the study extends beyond the approval period of one calendar year. This continuation must receive IRB review and approval before the research can continue.
3. Report any adverse events to the IRB Chair promptly. Adverse events are those which are unanticipated and impact the subjects during the course of this research; and
4. Notify the IRB office in writing when your research project is complete.

Please note that approved protocols are subject to monitoring by the IRB and that the IRB office has the authority to inspect research records associated with this protocol at any time. If you have questions about the IRB procedures or need any assistance from the Board, please contact Beth McTernan in 415 Whitehurst (phone: 405-744-5700, beth.mcternan@okstate.edu).

Sincerely,

Sue C. Jacobs, Chair
Institutional Review Board

189

APPENDIX C

PARTICIPANT CONSENT FORM

Participant Consent Form

The researcher is a doctoral student at Oklahoma State University, studying influences and barriers that affect career decision in computer technology fields. Your participation in the study is appreciated and valued. Participation will take about 15 minutes of your time. The goal of this study is to gain more understanding of the decision making process of selecting a major in a technology field. The study will identify influences and barriers that affect career decisions about computer technology careers, determine if these are different for males and females, and provide information to develop strategies to effectively recruit females into computer technology careers.

Please answer the questions on your own, honestly, and to the best of your ability. Read the following information about consent before completing the questionnaire.

Questionnaire Informed Consent

There are no known risks connected with this study.

The protection of participants is of greatest concern to the researcher and the following measures have been put into place to ensure the anonymity of all participants and the confidentiality of all data provided.

1. Questionnaires are submitted electronically to a WebSurveyor database with only an IP number for the computer that will be stripped from the databank, therefore making the submission completely anonymous.

2. Each questionnaire response will be assigned a number when submitted. This number will be used solely for data checking purposes.

3. The data will be stored in the electronic database and never printed.

4. The data will be deleted after completion of the analysis or within one year.

5. Submission of the questionnaire electronically will serve as your agreement to participate in this study and your consent to include your data in the analysis.

6. All data will be reported in aggregate only and no participant, his/her institutional affiliation, or any identifying characteristic will be reported or revealed.

Participation is voluntary and participants may discontinue the research activity at any time without reprisal or penalty by closing the Internet web site or online questionnaire. For information on participants' rights, contact Dr. Sue Jacobs, Oklahoma State University, IRB Chair, 415 Whitehurst Hall, Stillwater, Oklahoma, 405-744-1676. For information about the study, contact Judy Moody, Box 911, Muskogee, Oklahoma, 918-822-1455.

CLICK HERE TO CONTINUE   CLICK HERE TO EXIT

www.ingramcontent.com/pod-product-compliance
Lightning Source LLC
LaVergne TN
LVHW022312060326
832902LV00020B/3413

9 783639 018929